Gemstones and Dimes

By Sharon Dillon

Copyright 2018 Sharon Dillon
Daniel Wetta Publishing
Edited by Daniel Wetta

Please visit author blogsite at https://energywriter.me/
Author Webpage: https://danielwetta.com/sharondillon/

Other Books by Sharon Dillon
Echoes of Your Choices

Table of Contents	Page
Short Stories	1
Gemstone	3
Magic Dimes	10
McCarthy Goes Home	13
Missing: Beautiful Vixen	14
In the Beginning	15
Patty's New Chance	17
Rockin' Old Farts	20
Orders	23
Vietnam Widow	24
Along Came Smith	27
Postcard Mystery	34
Humor	72
A Halloween to Remember	73
A Mini-Con-Man	75
A New WMD (Weapon of Mass Destruction)	77
All Grown Up and...	79
An Exercise Program That Works	82
Blueberry Art: Bah! Humbug!	84
Oops, I Hit the Wrong Key	86
Christmas News Letter	88
Director of Capture Management	90
Dirt Fairy	91
Dragon Herding	93
Driver's License Woes	95
I Did It Wrong	97
How to Feel Like a Fool & Get Dishwasher Fixed	99
I'm An Artist	101

Life in the Cold Lane	102
Meeting Deadlines	103
Surprising News	106
No More Ads, Please	107
Officially Old	108
Pants on Fire	110
Tooth Fairy - Changed Tactics	112
Who Hid the Chocolate?	115
Twins - Oh No!	117
The Ruse	120
Reflections	121
My Greatest Honor of Military Life	122
He's a Marine, Mom. Be Cool	142
Daughters Tackle the Army	145
Thirteen Days in the Twilight Zone	147
Meant to Learn	153
The Way to Start Changing	156
Thoughts on Playing	158
Energy Writer is...	161
About the Author	164

Short Stories

2

Gemstone

Strange things were happening. Time seemed to be passing much too quickly. Technology was changing more rapidly than she could follow. What was happening?

Betty had a puzzle to solve. Where the puzzle would lead her was not clear. The only thing Betty knew was that to find the answer she had to drive through the desert.

She walked across the street and rented a compact car. After signing her name endless times on a digital pad, she downloaded a contract and instructions into her phone. Since Betty didn't know how far she would be traveling, she asked a disgruntled rental agent for paper instructions to purchase gas. He grudgingly printed the instructions and thrust them at her while giving her that look, the one reserved for older people who just didn't comprehend how the world worked without paper. "That's okay," she thought, "Someday he'll be old, too, and confused by whatever new technology younger people accept so easily."

After driving several hours, Betty spotted a gas station ahead. "Just in time," she said to herself. "It's time for a break." She pulled up to the refueling area; stepped out of the small, sleek, red car; stretched; glanced at the fuel pumps, and walked inside to refresh herself. After a mini-break with a cold energy drink from the automated machine, she walked outside and began to examine the pumps.

Betty always used the old-fashioned pumps at home. Those simply required her to slide her credit card into a slot, read the information screen, push a few buttons on the keypad and wait a few seconds until the screen indicated that her card had been accepted. She'd open the gas tank cover, insert the nozzle, squeeze the handle and let the gas flow until it stopped, then replace the nozzle, push a few more buttons and receive a printed receipt.

These pumps were different. They required a numerical pass code rather than a credit card. She opened the car door, pulled out her instructions and began to read:

"Type pass code 4549 and press enter.

"Select gas and press enter.

"Type security code and press enter."

Security code? Betty continued reading the instruction sheet and found no security code. She went back into the shop and looked for a person who could answer her question. She had been in such a hurry before that she hadn't noticed that no one was there. After walking up and down all the rows of snack and beverage machines, she found a sign beside an intercom on the wall. It read, "Questions? Press 637." She pressed those numbers and heard a light buzzing sound. A bored sounding voice said, "Yes? You have a question?"

"The fuel pump indicated that I have to enter a security code to refill my gas tank."

"That number is in the contract on your phone."

"That's pages and pages long. Why isn't it on the typed instructions?"

"It wouldn't be secure if it was on paper, now would it?"

"Okay, I'll go read it."

"Thank you for calling. Good-bye."

Betty walked back out to the car. She uncapped her cola drink, took a long swallow and picked up her phone. She scrolled through the contact list until she came to the contract, opened it and began to scan. She read all the subject headings, but never saw one that indicated it would contain a security code. Feeling more than a little frustrated, Betty stomped back inside to the wall communicator, punched in 637 and waited, drumming her fingers against the wall. After listening to that annoying buzzing sound for what seemed forever, the bored voice asked, "May I help you?"

Taking a deep breath to calm herself, Betty said, "Yes, please. I called a few minutes ago to obtain a security code to pump gas for my car. You told me I could find it in my contract. I read the whole contract and found no code. How am I supposed to refuel my car? I'm in the middle of the desert and there are no other gas stations in sight."

"Please be calm, ma'am. Get back in your car and drive west about five miles. You'll find a city built on a mesa. Park at the bottom and walk up the sidewalk." The voice then proceeded to give instructions about turning on this street and that one to arrive at the corporate offices. There she could show her contract and identification to the assistant and receive her security code.

Betty asked, "Why can't you just tell me the code?"

"I don't have access to that information."

"May I talk to someone who has access?"

"No ma'am. We have to see your contract."

"I can send you my contract."

"Sorry, ma'am. Anyone could have access to your contract."

"But, it will come from my phone."

"Anyone could have your phone. We need to know that this is you asking for the security code."

"I can send you my driver's license photo."

"No ma'am. Anyone with your phone can send your photo. You must come in person."

Betty walked away from the communication wall, muttering, "All this technology, and I have to walk up a mesa to show my face to a stranger to prove that I am me for just a few dollars in gas. It makes no sense." She climbed into her car and drove west. After a mile or so, she saw a mesa and was relieved to know that she was going in the right direction. As she came closer, she began to pick out features that looked like buildings, not only on top but also on the sides of the mesa.

Finally, she saw a huge parking lot that appeared to stretch around its entire base. A large sign read, "Commercial," with an arrow to the left and, "Residential," with an arrow to the right. She turned left and saw signs that directed her to various business zones. She found one that indicated petroleum and entered. As she drove along, she saw signage that indicated fuel companies. Finally, spotting one that matched the company name at the gas station where she had stopped, she turned into that lane and parked. After all that driving, she was delighted to find that the sidewalk was only about 10 feet away. Betty noted her parking lot and space number, put her identification and phone in her pocket, locked her purse in the trunk and picked up the remainder of her cola and a granola bar. She wanted to be prepared if she had to hike all the way to the top of this mesa.

Walking along, Betty noticed that the sidewalk was laid out in a zig-zag pattern to make the climb less intense. She saw that the low buildings were decorated in desert colors that blended with the mesa. Even though the mesa top was covered with streets and buildings, she could feel the sun warming her body and see sky that extended forever. What seemed strange was the lack of other people on the sidewalk. She could see people through shop and office windows. How did they move from place to place without using the sidewalk?

When she reached the top of the mesa, she saw a sign with directions to the building that she was seeking. "This is a good place for a break," she decided and sat down on a nearby bench. She took a long drink and then tore open her granola bar. Looking at her surroundings, Betty marveled that a desert garden and the architecture made the metropolis appear so natural. Her eyes lit upon a small piece of rose quartz on the sidewalk a few inches from her foot. It was clean but unpolished. She thought, "How beautiful! This will look great with my other rose quartz pieces at home." As she bent to pick it up, Betty blinked in surprise when the uncut stone changed into a faceted gem glowing in the sunlight.

A voice behind her commanded, "Don't touch it." Looking up Betty saw a man she knew standing there. Two others instantly appeared next to him. They were part of the mystery that had led her on this journey. The one called Steven said, "It may be a portal. If you pick up the gem, you may instantly leave here and find yourself in another time and place. Are you prepared to take that risk?"

"You're right. I'd better think about this before taking action."

The men disappeared as Betty sat on the bench staring at the rose quartz and trying to catch hold of the "what ifs" that were circling around in her brain. What if she picked it up and was transported to another time and place? What if she didn't pick it up and continued her uneventful life? What would be result of each choice? After several minutes, Betty decided that she couldn't take the risk and began walking back down the zig-zag sidewalk to the parking area.

By the time she reached her car, Betty decided she would like some adventure. She pulled another bottle of water and an energy bar from her cooler and locked the car again. This time she walked the slope with more energy in her step. A new adventure awaited her. She could hardly wait to begin.

Soon she reached the bench, sat down to catch her breath and saw only grass in front of her. The rose quartz was gone. How could it be gone? This was her opportunity to explore new and exciting adventures. It can't be gone! Betty slumped against the back of the bench and tried to comprehend what this all meant.

She heard footsteps and looked up. Steven approached and sat next to her. "So, you changed your mind and the stone is gone. What are you going to do now?"

"I don't know. I hesitated, then decided the adventure would be worth whatever the cost. If I lost my job, so what? The new adventure would provide for me."

"That is probably what would have happened, but you can't know for sure."

"What do I do now?"

"Go back to your life in the city. Maybe another opportunity will come along. The next time, you'll know that sometimes taking risks leads to a worthwhile adventure."

"When will that happen? What would be the adventure?"

I don't know," Steven said. "Maybe you need to take each step as it appears before you." His form began fading as she peered at him.

Betty sighed. She still was left with the frustrating problem of obtaining her security code. The bright desert sun seemed to shine now on a world mundane and washed out. She knew that each step back down the hill later would feel like a torturing retreat from the possibility of a better life.

But wait…perhaps she could learn to be more observant and sensitive to the messages of the world around her, even in the city? That thought put renewal in her step, even more than the energy bar. She looked around for the corporate door that would lead to her magic number for gas. She remembered seeing it before she sat down to eat her snack.

There it was to her left. Feeling like she had lost her last opportunity for adventure, Betty turned and walked slowly toward the office. Opening the door, she felt the air conditioning cool her body and her mood. A pleasant woman greeted her and asked, "Are you the woman who called about her security number a while ago?"

"Yes." As Betty dug into her shoulder bag, she said, "I hope this is in order. I already walked up that steep path twice."

"Oh, my goodness. You walked all that way? Twice? Oh, by the way, my name is Janet."

"How else was I to get here? Yes, I walked it twice. I walked up, rested, then realized I had forgotten my driver's license, so I had to walk back down to retrieve it."

"I'm so sorry you had to do that. Let's get your security number, and then I'll show you an easier way down the hill."

Soon all was in order, and Betty had not only her security number but also a pass code for a free tank of gas. As Janet walked Betty down the hall, they passed an elevator. She said, "You could have ridden up in this. You must have missed it. It's camouflaged somewhat to blend in with the natural beauty of the mesa."

"So, I can ride back down?"

"You can, but I'm offering another option, if you want to try it."

A few steps later, they approached what appeared to be another elevator door. Janet pressed the button. When the door opened, Betty saw that she was standing at the top of what appeared to be a giant playground slide. Not believing what she was seeing, Betty shook her head and took a step back.

"Are you up for an adventure? The landing is soft," Janet encouraged.

As she hesitated, Steven's voice echoed in Betty's head: "Maybe you need to take each step as it appears before you."

"Yes!" she exclaimed to Janet. "Are you coming with me?"

"I have to close the office, but then I'll take this way down to the parking lot." Janet showed Betty how to keep her feet and hands safely inside the slide, then she stepped back and pressed the down button. As Betty zipped downward, she shouted a reverberating, "Wow!" that certainly must have made Janet smile above.

When she reached the bottom of the slide, Betty eased herself up and pushed open the door to the parking lot. Feeling a rush of energy that she had not experienced in years, she thought, "The gemstone opportunity is gone, but I sure am going to be alert for new gemstones that come my way, whatever their appearance!"

Magic Dimes

The old man walked slowly up the steps of the planetarium, long since closed, but open this night to honor him, an astronaut from bygone days when Earth people still traveled to nearby planets. He wondered why school children were gathered to honor him when space travel was a thing of the past. The night sky was hidden behind the lights that illuminated the city at all times of day and night.

The population had grown so much that most of the Earth was covered with cities, and the remaining farm land was lit so agriculture work could continue day and night. These children had never seen the black night sky dotted with glowing specks of planets and stars. Their lessons contained only a passing reference to the men and women who had ventured into space to discover what lie beyond their own small existence.

As he walked, dimes, currency from the old days, jingled in his pocket. Nearing the abandoned buildings with their giant telescopes, the old man saw hundreds of children settling into their seats and heard teachers reminding them to be quiet so that they could hear the speaker when he arrived. He smiled as he remembered sitting in those same seats as a student to hear lectures about the planets. Occasionally, he had been lucky and was chosen to look through the giant telescope that allowed him to see the individual features of each tiny dot in the sky. Mars was red. Saturn had rings. He could see each of the planets in turn as the Earth rotated on its axis.

When he reached the podium, the old astronaut told the children how he and his classmates had come to this place to see the men and women who had ventured to Earth's moon. They had told their stories of exploring that celestial body and the long periods they had lived on a man-made orbiting space station. These adventures fostered dreams of someday travelling to far off galaxies. Their tales stirred his spirit and came alive in his dreams at night. He studied astronomy, engineering and mathematics diligently.

As he grew into a man, he was selected to be one of the fortunate few who left Earth's gravitational field to explore the planets of Earth's solar system and beyond. He drew 20 dimes, one for each trip into space, slowly out of his pocket. He explained how he had saved a shiny dime for each trip into space. He placed them in two stacks of ten on a narrow shelf above and behind his head so that the students could see them in the bright arena lights.

Just as the old astronaut was completing his speech, the lights dimmed, and the arena slowly enveloped in darkness. He told the children to look up into sky. If they watched carefully, they could see the planets on which he had walked. Enthralled by the astronaut's stories of a time that seemed long ago to them, yet just yesterday to him, they began leaving their seats and moving toward the dais in the unfamiliar dark. He cautioned them to be careful not to bump the frame holding his precious coins.

As the children surrounded him, realizing that he might lose the coins, precious mementos of a time that no longer existed, the man called out, "Be careful! You'll spill the dimes!" Not hearing him, the children continued pressing forward to the stage and began climbing upward. As he expected, a small foot bumped the ledge and a dime fell. Another dime fell and another. The man felt great sadness watching his life's accomplishments scatter to the ground. He knew he'd never be able to retrieve the dimes in this commotion.

From the depths of his sorrow, the man began to hear shouts of joy. As each coin fell slowly, more and more lights became dark; first nearby, then farther away and still farther until the night sky was black. Tiny specks of light began to pop into view. Earth's moon, Mercury, Venus, Mars, Jupiter, Saturn, Uranus, Neptune and even tiny Pluto shone among the other stars. The astronaut tried to settle the children back into their seats by telling them how each of Earth's primary planets was named after a god or goddess of ancient times.

Too excited to pay attention, the children kept climbing until they reached the top tier of the stadium and could see far, much farther than they had ever imagined, into the night sky.

They stopped moving and remained silent, focused on a view they had never witnessed. The magic of the twinkling sky held them spellbound. The old astronaut heard young voices here and there exclaim, "I want to visit that planet! I want to go to that star!"

That's when he knew why he was in this dark place, once again looking at a sparkling sky. He had lost his collection of dimes, but joy filled his soul. The dimes had summoned his destiny, bringing him to these children so he could provide them new views and expanded goals: gifts for a generation that had never known the joy of peering into the darkness where dreams could grow within their hearts.

McCarthy Goes Home

Corporal McCarthy sat on the edge of his bunk and allowed himself to daydream for the first time after twelve months in Viet Nam. Earlier this morning, Sarge had walked briskly into his squad tent and had said, "Get your gear together, Mac. You're going back to the world." Then they had a short, private talk about how to leave 'Nam behind and fit into family life.

When he had first arrived at the base camp, his squad leader had told him, "Keep your mind on the here-and-now. Those who daydream about home are the ones who don't go there." After just a few days on patrol, watching others come and go, some in body bags, Mac became a firm believer that being alert, even during sleep, was his only way to get home in one piece. He had a future there - one that didn't involve snipers, punji-pits and C-rats. He and Louisa were going to be married as soon as they could get the paperwork done. She'd already talked with the minister, and her parents had the VFW hall on stand-by for the reception. A short Huey ride would take him to Na Trang, then another to Tan Son Hut Airbase. That was where he would board the big silver bird that would take him to Ft. Lewis, Washington, for out-processing. Then he could go home.

Suddenly, he heard the Huey hovering overhead and gun fire in the bush on the far side of the camp. Mac grabbed his steel pot and weapon and ran toward the action. Sarge yelled, "To the chopper, Mac! Leave this to the rest of us!"

Mac ran back to his bunk, grabbed his gear and trotted toward the clearing where the Huey was landing. He watched the FNGs jump out, rifles at the ready, and head toward the sound of the action. Then he sprinted to the helicopter. Just as Mac reached the Huey, he felt a searing heat in his chest.

He whispered, "Louisa," and fell to the ground.

Missing: Beautiful Vixen

As Joe sat reading the newspaper, he opened it to the classified section. There in large print was a concisely written notice:

"Missing – beautiful, fit vixen with long, silky red hair. Likes to disguise her sly personality with a come-hither smile. Call 555-1212 if you see her."

Joe was in shock. The ad must be talking about Susan, his new girlfriend. She had appeared out of nowhere. She had beautiful, long red, wavy tresses that flowed nearly to her waist. Her dazzling smile made men fall instantly in love with her. She was tall with an athletic build and ran five miles every morning, returning to their apartment glistening with perspiration, but breathing evenly and easily. She loved to eat steak, but, sadly, she didn't know how to cook. That left Joe picking up the tab for frequent meals at high-cost steak houses. He didn't mind that, but Joe was learning the hard way that beneath Susan's lovely exterior lurked a prickly personality that quickly shifted to explosive anger. Joe had been trying to think of a way to break up with Susan that wouldn't make her anger flare in a frightening way.

Here was the answer! She was missing! Perhaps she had a form of amnesia. That would explain her reluctance to talk about her family. It would also account for her underlying anger. Fear and loss can do that to a person. Joe could return Susan to her family, knowing that she would be safe. This kind act would also give him a respite from her mercurial personality. If she recovered, they might resume their relationship in a calmer manner. Those thoughts filled Joe with hope.

Confidently, Joe walked to the counter, picked up his phone and dialed 555-1212. Imagine his surprise when the voice at the other end said, "County Zoo. May I help you?"

In the Beginning

In the beginning, the little girl read all the fairy tales and watched all the Disney movies. Her favorite stories ended with the handsome prince on the big white horse rescuing the beautiful princess from the fiery dragon, evil witch or wicked stepmother.

As the little girl became a teenager, she realized that she was not beautiful and certainly not a princess. Even so, she continued to dream of the handsome prince on the big, white horse rescuing her from the fiery dragons in her life. In high school, she met a few frogs, but none of them turned into a prince.

Finally, in her senior year, she met an ordinary guy, and he had a horse – not a big, white horse – but one that would carry her away to a new life. As the years passed, the guy's military career assured that she would visit some interesting locations. The young woman became the mother of a little prince and two little princesses. Meanwhile, the guy began turning into a dragon rather than a prince.

Fearing for their lives, the young mother and the children began walking through the forest to grandmother's house. Along the way, they met a big wolf, but he seemed to be a kind wolf. He convinced her that if she went with him, he would keep them safe from the dragon. Over the years, he took good care of the mother and the young royalty. He even convinced the woman that she was attractive. He was looking less like a wolf and more like a prince. But the wolf-prince had commitment issues. In addition, his eyes and teeth were beginning to gleam in the dark. By this time, the young prince and princesses had gone off to seek their fortunes. Without them to occupy her time and thoughts, the mother realized that she might not be a princess, but she felt that she deserved a real prince who would marry her and take her to his castle. She again began walking into the forest.

Eventually, she met a man who appeared to be a prince. He had no big white horse or palace, but the woman was impressed with his abilities and how far he had come from the cave where his family lived. They married and lived in a small and comfortable mini-castle. It wasn't long before the man began seeing enemies at the gate. He told the woman that only he could protect her from their evil ways, but his weapons were not effective. And, he was starting to croak when he talked. It sounded like, "Rib-good-ribbit-morning!"

"Uh-oh," she thought. "I've already escaped from a dragon and a wolf. Don't tell me I must flee again!" But, she knew that was the only answer. So, once again, she began walking through the forest.

She walked for several years. During this time, she realized that she was, indeed, beautiful and did not need a handsome prince with a big, white horse… because she was a real princess. That had to be so. Otherwise, how could she have given birth to three young royals?

She spent those years learning to feel comfortable wearing a crown and walking and talking like a princess. She became strong and learned to rule her queendom with a soft, yet firm hand.

Has she given up her dream of a handsome prince? Not entirely, but she knows that she will not be fooled by a pseudo-prince. She will wait until she meets a real prince who will recognize her royal birth, and they will share their royal duties.

Patty's New Chance

Tall and lean, wrapped in an over-sized gray wool sweater that smelled like Joey, Patty stood on her front porch, feeling the rough wood through her slippers while the wind whipped her blonde hair. She could taste the homemade chili that lingered on her tongue. Peering into the distance, she hoped to see what had made the sound. Whatever it was, the sound didn't belong in the silent, snowy night.

After Joey's death, Patty had moved to the country to get away from city noises and smells. She loved the fresh scent of growing plants and the colors that flooded her yard during the three mild seasons. She even loved the silent, shadowy expanse that spread before her eyes. But the sound....

While her vision was dim, Patty's hearing was sharp. This ability served her well, both as a musician and as help as her eyesight failed. The sound was almost like a baby crying. It was impossible to think that a baby would be out in this frigid weather. Perhaps it was a dog or cat in distress? Patty debated whether to go check, then decided she'd want someone to check on her little dog who was sleeping peacefully in front of the wood heater that supplemented her inadequate furnace.

Stepping back inside her mobile home, Patty replaced her slippers with snow boots and pulled her coat over the heavy sweater. "Come on, Sam, we need to go looking for a lost pet. Your vision is better than mine. Perhaps together we can find it quickly."

Sam bounded down the steps as Patty eased her body along the railing. Earlier, the sun had melted the snow on the steps, but the remaining water had frozen, turning each step into a mini ice-skating rink. Once she reached the ground, Patty called to Sam and began walking in the direction of the sound. Other than the crying sound, the night was silent. All the birds and woodland creatures had found shelter for the night. Perhaps they were watching Animal Planet on their tiny televisions. The thought made Patty smile to herself.

The wind and snow made the walk seem to last forever. As she looked back at her home and its lights, Patty realized that they had walked much farther than she had planned. Yet, no matter how far they walked, the crying sound seemed to be a bit more distant.

Knowing they were so close, Patty had no thought of abandoning the search. Soon her hands began to seize up inside her gloves. She could feel her toes curling to keep warm. How much farther? Was the animal crawling away from her faster than she could walk? Or was it a baby whose mother was carrying it down this snow-covered road?

Just as she crested the small hill, a voice almost like Joey's said, "Lie down, Patty." She must be imagining things. Joey was dead and even if he could communicate with her, why would he tell her to lie down in the deep snow? Wouldn't he tell her to return to the safety and warmth of her mobile home?

Sam began barking. Patty told him to be quiet. "We can't hear the sound if you are making so much noise." Sam stopped barking and began tugging on the bottom of her coat. Patty stood where she was, listening for the sound. She no longer heard the crying. Instead, she heard, "Patty, lie down, right here, right now." Sam was jumping up and down forcing her to look at him. He then lay down in the snow and curled up.

Patty said, "Sam, get up. I don't hear the sound anymore. Perhaps whatever it was found shelter." Suddenly, the sound returned and seemed to come from under the large spruce tree next to the road. Patty walked across the road and knelt to peer under the low branches. The sound continued. Patty crawled all the way under the low-hanging branches. Sam crowded in beside her.

The voice returned, "Patty, stay here a little while."

Getting no answer, Patty closed her eyes in frustration. Just then she heard a boom. She rushed back to the road and saw flames reaching for the sky as another boom shattered the night. They were coming from the direction of her home. "Oh, shit! After waiting all those years for Joey to buy me a house, I finally got my own home and it goes up in flames! Everything is lost!"

With tears streaming from her eyes and freezing on her cheeks, Patty urged Sam to come out from under the tree. They began walking down the road. Almost frozen and struggling, Patty and Sam reached the nearest house. She didn't have to awaken them. They were moving around in their yard trying to figure out what they had heard.

"Please, call 911. My house exploded!" Patty shouted.

Soon Patty and Sam were wrapped in warm blankets as the fire trucks screamed their way to what was left of her home. The neighbors drove her back to the commotion. Numbly, she answered the chief's questions about following the crying sound and how luck played a part in their safety. She kept the voice to herself. That was something she would need to think about over the next few days as she tried to figure out what to do next.

The Red Cross offered her a hotel room, some clothes and food. That was a huge relief. At least she didn't have to worry about tomorrow and the next day. This would give her time to discuss her situation with her family and try to decide what to do about replacing her home and her belongings. Those weren't much as far as the world goes, but many were precious gifts from Joey's mother. Rose had been a loving, surrogate mom after her own mother had passed and had provided for Patty in her will. That's how she had been able to buy the mobile home.

The fire chief came to Patty's hotel and told her that the fire was caused by a tiny crack in the furnace gas pipe. Since the pipe was outside the house and the wind was blowing away from her mobile home, she would not have smelled the gas in time to evacuate.

Sunday came and Patty found a ride to church. Her car was gone too. As they rode along, her friend said, "Patty, you must have had an angel watching out for you and Sam. You got out just in time."

"You're right. We're safe even if everything is gone."

"Just last week you said you'd like to start over. Here's your chance."

"I'll think about that," Patty said softly.

She heard Joey chuckle and whisper, "I love you, Babe."

Tears ran down her face as she silently said, "Thank you, Joey."

Rockin' Old Farts

"Jerry, stop dancing to the elevator music. We're on our way to discuss a merger. These people need to believe that we're serious about their proposal."

"You know, Tom, you've always been a tight-ass. I'm tired of all this corporate nonsense. I quit."

"You're nuts. You're 50, have a mortgage, three kids and two dogs depending on you. Now straighten your tie and get ready to negotiate."

"No, it's past time that I follow my dream. I'm going to get the band together and hit the road."

Tom shook his head as Jerry dumped the contents of his briefcase onto the elevator floor and danced down the hallway. Bending to pick up the mess, Tom muttered, "Jerry's nuts. He's going to crash and burn. Quitting like this, he won't even get severance pay." But as he quickly reviewed the negotiating points in his head, he realized that he secretly envied Jerry's determination.

Jerry cleaned out his desk and drove his minivan home. He told his wife, "May, I've quit my job. I'm going to get the band back together and hit the road."

She stared at him a few moments. "What's wrong with you? Did you hit your head?

"Yes, I was hit on the head with reality. If I don't follow my dream now, I never will."

Raising her face to the ceiling, May muttered, "God, talk some sense into this idiot."

***

Jerry called his college friends and asked them to meet at his house at 8 p.m. After a silent supper (because even the kids and dogs refused to interact with him), Jerry set out chips and made sure that the beer was cold. As each of Jerry's four friends arrived, they asked what the excitement was about.

"Not yet. I'll tell you when everyone's here."

By 8:15 everyone was there. Steve, in his softball uniform; Tony, still in his suit with his tie askew; Gil wearing his usual

Dockers and polo shirt; and Ed in his usual sweats and dirty sneakers.

"Let's get started," Steve said, "I need to get home and wash off this home-plate dirt."

"Yeah," Tony added, "My wife is really pissed that I'm getting home late again."

"Okay. Here's the deal. Today I quit my job to pursue my lifetime dream of performing. I'm asking you to quit your jobs so we can get the band going again."

"Are you out of your mind?" Gill shouted. "We have responsibilities – and we're old!"

"The Rolling Stones are older than we are. Paul McCartney is older. Look at Tony Bennett. He must be 105, and the girls are still swooning for him."

"Jerry has a point," Ed said. "We're 50. It's now or never. Let's do it."

"Okay. When?" Tony asked.

"Tomorrow at 10a.m., here in my garage. Bring your instruments."

***

"This rehearsal was great, guys," Jerry said. A couple more, and we'll be ready to hit the road. I'll call a friend who knows an agent. He'll set up our gigs and handle the money."

"The money?" Tony asked. "I put all my assets in my wife's name so when we go broke the bank can't take the house."

"Just wait. You'll see. Hey, I have a great idea. Let's not pretend to be young. Let's go with who we are."

***

Two weeks later, the Rockin' Old Farts, with Jerry as lead singer, played the county fair. Next came a pre-game show for the local AA baseball championship. Soon they were playing in neighboring cities and wowing the crowds. Middle-aged women and even 20-somethings were filling the seats.

A recording contract followed with a video that included motorcycles and gyrating young women. The video made the top ten. Soon they were playing in Cleveland, Memphis, and New

Orleans. Each show was a sell-out. Ticket prices went higher and higher.

Then came Chicago, Los Angeles and the *coup-de-gras*, Madison Square Garden. Foot-high letters across the marquee announced, "Rockin' Old Farts tonight at 8 p.m. Sold out performance."

The men were now wearing sequin suits and their long hair fell over their eyes. "Ladies and Gentlemen, Madison Square Garden is proud to present "Rockin' Old Farts with lead singer, Jerry."

"Jerry! Jerry! Jerry!" the crowd chanted.

***

Ding!

"Jerry. Jerry. Jerry! What, you in some kind of daydream? We've reached the conference floor. You fell asleep on the elevator. Come on, get with it!"

"Huh?" Jerry said, shaking his head as if to get rid of cobwebs.

"What the heck? You just yelled, 'Hello, New York!'"

Orders

The commander stood at the front of the assembled warriors. The stage was bare except for the United States flag, the battalion flag and the commander. What would he tell these men and women whom he had come to know and respect? How could he tell them that most would not return from their mission? He closed his eyes and opened his mind, waiting for the words to flow.

The group shifted their weight from side to side, occasionally wiggling their toes and blinking their eyes, as they awaited their orders. No sound or movement was visible. Scuttlebutt had been flying around the base for a couple of days. They had been anticipating a dangerous mission and were certain a decision had been made. Now they would learn the details.

In the third row stood a young woman who had come to regard her commander as more than just a superior officer. He had earned her respect. Her thought colors were agitated as she listened to his words and envisioned the upcoming battle. She turned those images and thoughts in her imagination, anticipating what actions would unfold around her. She visualized the battle scene and her role as team leader. Could she bring them all back safely? Doubts clouded her mind. The opposing force was larger than theirs and knew the terrain much better. She pushed her fears aside so that she could concentrate on the commander's instructions.

He detailed each team's assignments: attack, defend, flank, provide supplies and, as always, medical/retrieval. The commander ended his instructions by saying, "Keep your heads down and your powder dry."

Each team member knew he was repeating age-old instructions, good advice to anyone facing danger.

As the troops began quietly filing out of the building, the commander sighed and made his exit in silence.

Vietnam Widow

Looking out her living room window, Luanne watched an Army sedan pull into the driveway. That image told her all she needed to know – Joe had been killed in action. Tears welled up in her eyes and a sob escaped her throat as she opened the door. The two officers were deep in shadow as the sun flooded the front yard. Luanne whispered, "I understand," and invited them in and offered them coffee. Comprehending her need to do what was normal, the officers accepted. Luanne held back her tears while she busied herself making coffee.

Over the fresh, hot beverage, the officers related what they knew. Joe had been leading a squad patrolling the jungle not far from the Mekong River. Being alert, he had spotted what appeared to be a Vietcong tunnel opening. As his men opened the covering, another cover silently lifted behind them, and four Vietcong rained rifle-fire into the squad, killing Joe and two others and injuring four more. Joe's heroic actions as he returned fire earned him a Bronze Star. The officers said that they hoped to have the paperwork completed in time to present the medal at the funeral along with the flag that would cover his coffin. As they left, the officers told Luanne that her husband's body would be arriving within a few days.

Luanne was grateful that her three small children were playing in the park and that they didn't see the officers. She wanted to tell them in her own way and needed a few minutes to compose herself and determine what words she would use. How do you tell three preschoolers that their father was never coming home again? They had learned to print their names just so they could sign her daily letters to Joe. Joe was elated when he received the first letter which the children had signed in their lopsided printing.

All too soon, Susan, her next-door neighbor arrived with her children and Luanne's. The kids were shouting, "Mommy, Mommy, guess what we did today," as they propelled their way into the kitchen. Suddenly, their voices silenced when they saw her face. Something horrible must have happened to make Mommy look so sad. The kids slowly approached their mother with arms open wide.

They didn't know what had happened. They only knew she needed hugs.

Susan noticed the extra cups on the table and asked, "Did they come today?" Luanne nodded and couldn't stop the tears from falling on her babies' soft, shiny hair. Susan said she'd leave them alone and return after calling their pastor. Even though Susan knew things were not always right with Luanne and Joe, she knew how she'd feel if Bob didn't come home from the war. She felt lucky that Bob had returned safely from Vietnam just a few months ago, shortly before Joe left.

Luanne sat the children on the sofa and gently told them that their brave daddy had gone to live with the angels. They knew what that meant, because their pet rabbit had died a few weeks previously. Solemnly, they accepted her words and hugged her again before going to their rooms.

Just then the doorbell rang. Susan had returned by this time and let the visitors in. Luanne's neighbors had watched from their windows and waited to give her time to tell the children before they came to offer their condolences. Being Army wives themselves, they all watched to see whom the military sedan would visit. Luckily for them, the dreaded sedan had not yet visited their homes. As they comforted Luanne, they kept their thoughts of Joe's unusual behavior to themselves. The women determined who would provide which meals and do the laundry before the out-of-state relatives arrived. Cleaning the house was not necessary because Luanne was an immaculate housekeeper.

About that time, the pastor arrived and prayed with the women, not only for Joe's soul, but that all their husbands would remain safe. Susan stayed with Luanne while she called her and Joe's parents.

Tearful days and long sleepless nights passed. Relatives arrived. Arguments ensued over the funeral arrangements. Joe's parents wanted him buried in the family plot in Kansas. Luanne's parents thought he should be buried in their family plot in Missouri. Luanne insisted that since he loved the Army so much he should be buried in the nearest veterans' cemetery. Finally, they all agreed, somewhat grudgingly, to Luanne's choice.

The funeral day was warm and sunny with flowers blooming all over the cemetery. Luanne knew that Joe would love this spot. The sight of the flag-draped coffin turned her insides to soup. She prayed that she'd get through this horrible day without vomiting on the flowers that banked the grave. The children sensed the solemnity of these events and behaved like small adults.

Finally, the pastor finished the service. He had kept his personal thoughts about Joe to himself. He focused on Joe's acts of bravery in battle. As the bugler played "Taps," not a single eye remained dry. Collectively, their thoughts encompassed not only Joe, but all brave men and women who had given their lives for the United States.

Days passed in a haze as Luanne said farewell to the relatives returning to their homes. She even found herself resuming her usual routine. Taking care of the children was her most important task. Luanne reminded herself that no matter how depressed she felt, the children still needed her love and attention.

One day while checking the mail, Luanne saw an envelope from the insurance company. She sighed a breath of relief, knowing that she could start making plans for her family's future. Opening the envelope, she discovered the check was far more than she expected. Luanne sat with her coffee and listed the ways the insurance could help her little family. Ideas included paying off the mortgage on their house, going to college so she could get a good-paying job, and quality day-care for the children. She would be the woman she knew she could be. She would be a loving mother who responded to her children's needs without worrying that her husband would feel slighted. She no longer had to listen to criticisms of her housekeeping, her appearance, her parenting skills or anything else Joe could imagine.

Luanne suddenly realized that the death of a spouse was not the end of the line, but the start of a new journey. She gasped as an unthinkable thought bubbled to the front of her mind. She was free!

Along came Smith…

"Bye, Mike! What a fun weekend! See you at school tomorrow."

"Angie, need some help with your camping gear?"

"Sure do, Dad."

"Mr. Lewis, let me get that rear door for you. It tends to stick."

"ANGIE! What happened to you? Mike, stay right where you are!" Mr. Lewis frantically dug into his jeans' pocket and pulled out his phone.

"911, may I help you?"

"Get an officer over to 332 Elm Street right now! I'm reporting an assault …"

No, Dad! What's wrong with you?"

"Your name and location, sir?"

Mike moves forward, "Mr. Lewis, what's wrong?"

"Stay exactly where you are! Don't move a muscle until the police get here! Angie, you stay put too."

"Dad? What's wrong?"

"Sir, I need your name and location."

"Mr. Lewis…"

"Robert Lewis, 332 Elm Street."

"Your emergency, sir?"

"I told you there has been a sexual assault. The victim and perpetrator are right here. Get someone over here right now."

"Mike didn't do anything to me, Dad! Please relax."

"Do you need an ambulance, sir?"

"Mr. Lewis, what…?"

"Yes! Now stop talking and get the police and ambulance here RIGHT NOW!" Mr. Lewis crammed the phone back into his pocket and glared at Mike, "Stay put!"

"I didn't do anything to your daughter, Mr. Lewis. I was sick until about 10 minutes ago.

"That's right, Dad. What makes you think…?"

Mrs. Lewis runs out the front door and across the lawn to where the van is stopped in the street. "What's going on? Bob, what are you yelling about?"

"Look at your daughter! This animal attacked her."

"What?"

"No, Mom and Dad. Mike didn't do anything to me."

"Angie, do you think I'm stupid?"

"Of course not, Dad, but I don't know what you are angry about."

"Susan, look at your daughter's neck. That animal standing there did that to her."

"Did what, Dad? What's wrong with my neck?"

"You have bruises all over the left side of your neck. I was young once, I know what that means – hickeys. Susan call Pastor Ray and demand that he come over immediately."

"Hickeys? Let me see," Mrs. Lewis demanded. "Oh, my God! Angie, go to your room. I thought we had this talk, but it looks like we need to do it again." As she spoke Susan reached for her phone and speed dialed the pastor.

Just then everyone looked up as a police patrol car pulled up to the curb. Two officers jumped out and ran to the gathered family. "Where's the victim? Who was injured? Is she inside the house? Why isn't someone with her?"

"Here's the victim, officer." Mr. Lewis turned Angie so the officer could see the left side of her neck. "See all the hickeys on her neck?"

Officer Smith reached for her radio. "EMT Unit 5, you can turn off your sirens, but continue to the site. A teen girl has severe bruising and may require first aid."

"Ten-four. We'll be there in five."

"Roger. Out."

Officer Smith turned to the family and Mike. "When I was young, I was not a 'nice' girl, if you get my drift. I know a hickey bruise when I see one. And those aren't hickey bruises. See the straight lines on the bottom of each bruise? They are obviously very fresh."

Mr. Lewis stepped forward and looked closer, "Okay, I see your point. But, there was still some violence going on. Arrest this young man immediately."

"Not until we get the story straight, sir."

Officer Jones joined the conversation. "Let's move up on the porch where we can sit down. I think it's pretty obvious we're going to be here a while, and the longer we stand out here in the street, the more people are going to wander over here."

Everyone's eyes followed his hand pointing to one or two people standing at the edge of each lawn with all eyes focused on them. As their faces registered shock, the little group turned and began walking up the drive way. Jones spoke up again. "Who owns this piece of crap van?"

Mike raised his hand, "Mine, sir."

"Well, park it properly and turn off the engine. I'll stay here with you so you won't decide to drive away. I don't feel like chasing a stupid kid through the streets today."

"No, sir-r-r-r," Mike began trembling and had difficulty opening the driver's door.

Soon all were seated on the porch swing or steps. Officer Smith announced, "I'll interview the victim. Jones, take the alleged perpetrator down to the other end and get his story."

"Okay. Let's go, Mike."

Just then the ambulance pulled up, and the EMTs ran across the lawn with their emergency kits and stopped at the porch's edge. "Where's the injured girl?"

Angie timidly raised her hand, still not sure what was going on. The medics looked at the bruises and saw there was no blood. They followed their standard procedure to verify that she was well and had no more injuries. Filling out their reports and handing one to Mrs. Lewis, the EMTs headed back to their ambulance. Their chuckles drifted back up to the group.

In the meantime, Jones listened carefully and took notes as Mike described their trip home. "Then what happened?" the group heard Officer Jones ask. They all strained their ears to hear Mike's story. Mr. Lewis stood up and began walking toward the officer and boy.

"Let's stay focused right here, Mr. Lewis. Angie, it's obvious that these bruises are very new," Officer Smith said. "Tell us everything that happened on your way home from your retreat."

"Just a moment, please. Bob, this was Pastor Ray. He hasn't left the retreat center yet, but will stop over as soon as he gets back to town."

"Now that's out of the way, let's return to Angie's story," Officer Smith said. "Angie, don't leave out a single detail."

"Mike drove me to the retreat center since he has this big van to carry everything in. We were carrying food as well as our gear. I rode back with him too. We left about 10:00, and bouncing over the pot holes made him sick. Mike pulled over and asked me to drive. I climbed into the driver seat and Mike stretched out on the middle seat, moaning and groaning. After a few minutes, Mike yelled for me to stop. I did. He dove out the door and vomited and vomited and vomited. When he finally stopped, I gave him a towel and a bottle of water. When his stomach settled down, he climbed back into the middle seat and I drove off."

"That explains Mike's disgusting odor," Mrs. Lewis commented.

"Back to your story, Angie," Officer Smith said.

"Nothing else, I drove until we arrived at the edge of town. Mike said he felt better and finished driving me home."

"Nice story, Angie. But, it doesn't explain your bruises. Did you stop on the way home to play 'suffocation?'"

"What's that?" Mr. Lewis asked.

"It's a game where one person chokes the other who has a plastic bag over her head while having sex. They say it makes orgasm more intense. But, often it leaves a person dead."

"Oh, how awful," Mrs. Lewis said. "Bob, did you know about this?"

"I've heard of it, but certainly didn't think our Angie would do that."

"No, no, no! We didn't do anything like that. We didn't even kiss. Mike is… Oops!"

"Mike is gay?" Officer Smith asked.

"Please don't tell anyone. His parents are very strict, and he'd have problems if they knew."

"I have no reason to tell them. Mr. and Mrs. Lewis, can you keep the secret? Mike has to be the one to tell his parents. It's like a rite of passage. If someone else tells, family dynamics will be messed up for a long time, perhaps forever."

The Lewises both shook their heads yes.

"Since nothing happened between you and Mike, Angie, I want you to go over the whole weekend. Tell us everything. Don't let anything out."

Angie began her story in long, boring detail until she came to Saturday night. As they all sat around the campfire, the boys began a marshmallow eating contest. "Mike won, just beating out Pastor Ray by two. They both looked a bit under the weather when we walked back to the dorm. This morning we got up, dressed and headed to the dining hall. This time, the boys wanted to see who could eat the most bacon. Mike won again by one slice. Pastor Ray was disappointed he didn't win."

"This explains why you were driving, but not how you got bruised," Mr. Lewis said.

"Well, my neck got a bit sore from the seat belt, but it didn't hurt much. I don't think that did it."

"Let's go check the van," Officer Smith called to Officer Jones. As he approached, she asked if he got anything interesting from Mike.

"Just some weird story about marshmallows and bacon," Jones chuckled. "Whatever that means."

Jones opened the driver door and began inspecting the area. "Whoa. Look here," he said as he pointed under the seat showing Smith that it had been nailed into place. "I think we have our bruiser. Angie's short, right?"

"Yeah, so?"

"And Mike is tall?"

"So?"

"This seat is positioned for Mike's comfort," Officer Jones explained. "If Angie was driving she'd have to sit on the edge of the seat to reach the pedals. Today's kids automatically use their seat belts, even if they are uncomfortable. She pulled the seat belt around her and fastened it. As she drove the seat, belt kept pulling against her neck and bruising her."

"Wouldn't she have checked the pain?"

"Not necessarily. Pressure bruising isn't painful, so it isn't noticeable until the person sees the bruise. So, Angie wouldn't have realized she was bruised until she looked in the mirror. I'll bet she has bruises on her right hip too."

"Let's check it out and head back for lunch."

"Angie, Mrs. Lewis, let's step into your nearest bathroom," Officer Smith said.

They all walked into the guest bathroom that was just off the entry way. "Please undo your shorts enough for me to see your right hip bone."

"Why?"

"Just do it. What we see there will probably resolve this whole situation."

Angie unbuttoned her shorts and slid the right side down a couple of inches.

"Just as I thought, your hip is bruised too."

"What? Where did that come from?"

"I'll explain in a minute when we get everyone back together. I only want to tell this story once." (*Until I get back to the station,* Smith said under her breath.)

"Okay, everyone's here and clued in on various parts of the story," Officer Smith announced. "Let me put all the pieces together to solve the mystery. Mike is not at fault; neither is Angie. Mike was too sick to drive, so Angie drove almost all the way home. Because Mike's van is, shall we say, not in the best shape, he had nailed the driver seat so it was comfortable for him. Angie, being shorter, had to sit on the edge of the seat to reach the petals. Being a conscientious young lady, she used the seat belt. Because of the angle at which she sat, the seat belt crossed her neck rather than her chest. Each bump would have caused a new pressure bruise, indicated by these straight lines under each one. She has matching bruises on her right hip where the seat belt stretched to the clip."

"Oh, that's so good to hear," Susan Lewis sighed.

Bob joined in, "Mike I owe you an apology."

"That's okay, sir, you were just being a good dad."

"Before this mutual admiration society gets too involved, we have instructions: Mike, Officer Jones is issuing you a summons for operating an unsafe vehicle, and it lists all the repairs you need to make. As soon as you fix that piece of garbage, take it to a dealer for a safety inspection. Bring the summons and certification to court. The judge will verify that all the repairs have been made and discharge the summons.

"Mr. Lewis, go to your dealer and buy a seat belt extender that Angie has to carry in her purse whenever she's out with friends. Should this happen again, the extender will hold the seat belt into proper position and avoid this bruising.

"Mrs. Lewis, go through your makeup and find some concealer to cover up the bruises. We don't want her to go to school looking like she wrestled with Count Dracula."

Just then Pastor Ray pulled into the driveway. "Sorry, I'm late folks. For some reason, breakfast didn't agree with me, and I had to shower and change clothes before I left the retreat center. My wife is going to be angry. Those clothes smell like marshmallows and bacon!"

Postcard Mystery

Mary Ellen was hurrying to leave the house, putting the final touches on her makeup, giving special attention to her concealer, foundation and eye shadow. Sally, her adult daughter, pulled into the driveway and honked. As Mary Ellen grabbed her purse, she slid a small blue item into the side pocket.

After a short drive to Virginia Beach and a relaxing ferry ride across the Elizabeth River, she and Sally were walking, talking and enjoying the unique architecture of Portsmouth's Old Town. Sally was careful not to mention the too-heavy makeup, knowing what lie under it. She worried, but she understood that her mother had to make her own decisions.

After a delicious lunch and another short stroll, they stopped for ice cream. Mary Ellen suggested, "Why don't we buy a post card for Grandma? You know how she loves historic buildings." They picked out a pretty card, and Mary Ellen wrote, "These are just some of the beautiful buildings you'll see when you visit us this summer." As she dropped the postcard into the mailbox, something small and blue went in with it.

***

As Susan walked to the mailbox, she noticed that the Bradford Pear trees were starting to show buds and daffodils and that the irises were beginning to pop through the soil. "What a beautiful day! Spring is almost here. All is well with the world," she thought.

When she opened the mailbox, Susan knew immediately that all was not well with the world. She noticed a blue postcard on top of the stack. It showed two dolphins jumping majestically above a calm sea. The words, "Port Aransas," scrolled across the bottom of the card.

Someone was in trouble. It could only be one of three women from her high school days. She knew what she would find when she turned the card over: "Pals forever, Susan, Robin, Elise and Tiger." Tiger was actually a very shy Mary Ellen who wanted to be tough and adopted the name of a fierce animal.

Instantly, Susan's mind carried her back to that day in April 1985 when their senior class spent spring break in Port Aransas, TX.

Though they had not been close in high school, circumstances threw them together for those four sunny days, swimming in the Gulf of Mexico, tasting Tex-Mex food for the first time and eyeing all those gorgeous young men on the beach.

On their last night on the beach. they had vowed to be friends forever and then sealed their intentions by writing the postcards. They had each bought one of the distinctive dolphin cards, and they worded them identically and vowed to keep them always. If anyone had a situation that she couldn't handle on her own, she would send a dolphin card to one of the others. The one receiving the card was to find the others and rush to the aid of the sender.

Only one problem blocked this rescue: The sender didn't add her name and address or phone number. How could she know which of them, Robin, Elise or Tiger, needed help? And, where were they? After high school, Susan, Robin and Elise had gone to different colleges, and Tiger had married a soldier and traveled around the world. What was his name? And, how did the sender get her address? Susan had moved several times after high school and had not kept in contact with anyone from her hometown, except her parents.

Susan walked slowly home, trying to think of a solution to this obvious dilemma. When she entered her small and comfortable condo, she went directly to the kitchen and began brewing a pot of chamomile-lavender tea. This problem would require some quiet thought. She sipped her tea and asked Spirit for guidance. As Susan sat quietly, an idea formed. She went online and searched for their high school alumni association.

Within hours, she received a reply with the email addresses for Elise and Robin, but none for Tiger. Susan began to suspect that is was Tiger who had summoned help. But, how could she find her? After emailing Robin and Elise, Susan studied the post card for more clues. She noticed that the postmark was from Portsmouth, but she could not decipher the state. That part of the postmark was on a black Texas logo.

Susan decided to try Google again. She went to the web and typed in a search for "cities named Portsmouth." After skimming through several pages of search results, Susan found Portsmouth in Virginia, Rhode Island, New Hampshire, Ohio and Michigan. Was

Tiger still married to the soldier? What was his name? And, which Portsmouth could be her current home?

After this search, Susan went back to her email and found messages confirming that both Robin and Elise were fine. Robin recalled that Tiger had a brother. Perhaps they could find him, and he would give them her address. Another alumni search showed that Tiger's brother, Bart, was listed as still living in their home town. Robin lived there, too.

Susan sipped another cup of tea and pondered how to word the email to Bart. She couldn't just write, "I received an unsigned postcard that may have come from Mary Ellen, and, by the way, is she safe?" Finally, she came up with a reasonable explanation for Bart about wanting to find an old friend.

Bart responded that Tiger was living in Hampton, Virginia. Her husband had retired from the Army and was now a civilian employee at nearby Fort Eustis. Portsmouth was just across the Hampton Roads Bridge-Tunnel and a short ferry ride from Norfolk's Waterside District. Now Susan knew why she had been chosen to receive the postcard. She lived in Williamsburg, only about 30 miles away. That raised a new question: Why hadn't Tiger just telephoned?

Susan promptly emailed Robin and Elise and told them what she had learned and informed them that she would go to Hampton to try to find Tiger. Robin and Elise conferred by phone, then responded that Susan should wait until the next day when they would be flying into the Newport News-Williamsburg airport.

Robin and Elise's flights arrived within an hour of each other. After hugs and small lies that "you haven't changed a bit since high school," they went into the airport coffee shop and brainstormed ideas for finding Tiger.

Susan said, "I found Tiger's husband, MSgt (Ret.) Martin Schuman, listed in the Hampton Roads phone book, but I didn't call him. Martin may be abusing Tiger. I don't want to cause more trouble."

They debated why Tiger would have waited so long to contact them if that was the situation. "An abused wife often justifies her husband's behavior for 'the sake of the children,'" Elise suggested. They all nodded sadly.

After studying the Hampton Roads atlas, they drove to a spot just up the street from a small and tidy looking bungalow. The yard was neat and full of flowers.

"This has to be the place." Robin said. "Remember how Tiger worked at the greenhouse during high school and brought frequent bouquets to Ms. Snyder and Ms. Bowman?"

Not knowing Martin's schedule, they decided to keep watch on the house until they could be sure that they would not run into him when they approached Tiger. After an hour, a middle-aged man left the house with a brief case. Thinking that perhaps that it was Martin returning to work after lunch at home, they waited for him to drive away, and then they walked briskly up to the house and rang the doorbell.

Tiger opened the door wearing heavy make-up and sunglasses. They yelled, "Surprise!"

"Who is it, Mary Ellen?" shouted a loud voice from the bathroom.

"Just some old school friends, Hon. They're in town for the Women in Aviation conference and just stopped by to say hello," Tiger responded, perhaps too quickly.

"We're sorry," Robin whispered. "If this is a bad time, we can come back later or meet you at the mall for coffee."

But Martin entered the room and heard her. He said, "You're here. Come on in. What a busy day! First the window salesman, now you."

The next hour passed very uncomfortably while Tiger made coffee and the four women exchanged high school memories. They began with compliments about the lovely front yard. They scrambled to invent credible answers to Martin's questions about their connection to aviation. None of them mentioned the postcard or their vows to aid one another. When the conversation lagged and slowed to an awkward halt, the women announced that they had to leave. They said their good-byes. As they hugged Tiger, each one quietly repeated Susan's phone number in her ear.

***

"Why did those women stop here asking questions about our personal business?" Martin demanded.

"I told you. They're in town for a conference. They didn't ask any personal questions."

"Yes, they did. They asked what places we've visited and how many kids we have. How did they know where we live?"

"Those are just general interest questions. I suppose they found us on the internet. Everything is out there for the world to find with little effort," Mary Ellen responded.

"What made them decide to visit after all these years?"

"Why not? Don't you ever think about looking up old friends?"

"It just seems suspicious. Don't you think so?"

"No. Remember, Elise said she still lives in my hometown, so she probably ran into Bart and asked about us. Maybe when he told her that we live close to their conference center, it just made sense to stop and surprise me with a hello."

Martin seemed mollified by that answer. "Well, they'd better not cause us any problems."

"Why would they? They're just here for a couple days," Mary Ellen asked. To herself, she silently repeated the phone number each had whispered in her ear so she could remember it.

"We'll see," Martin relented. "I'm hungry. Fix supper. Make a pot roast with those little roasted potatoes."

"Martin, that takes about two hours to cook, and the meat isn't thawed. What about some hamburgers?"

"I want pot roast. Make me a hamburger to keep me going until you get your sorry butt in gear to cook real food."

***

As Susan drove back to Williamsburg, the women discussed their impressions of the visit. "Did you notice that Mary Ellen kept her sunglasses on the whole time we were there?"

"Yes," Elise responded, "And you could tell Martin was not happy we were there."

"He could have been stressed from the sales call, as he mentioned," Robin suggested, "but you would think that a visit from his wife's old friends would have pushed price quotes out of his mind for a few minutes."

"It was more than that," Susan replied. "I remember that Don acted the same way before our divorce. So, what are we going to do about it?"

"We can't just kidnap her," Robin said. "We'll have to find a way to talk to her when Martin isn't home."

Their conversation continued off and on throughout the evening, circling the situation without any solutions becoming evident. Finally, Robin and Elise, exhausted after a long day of travel and the Mary Ellen encounter, retreated to the twin beds in Susan's extra bedroom.

***

About 2 a.m., Susan's cell phone buzzed on her nightstand. Rousing herself from a dream of whisking Mary Ellen to safety, she mumbled, "Hello."

A tiny voice she could barely hear said, "It's me. Martin is asleep now. He's really angry that you stopped in for a visit."

"We can be there in an hour. Will you be ready to go?"

"Not yet. I'm trying to get some paperwork done that will assure a post-Martin income. I haven't worked in all these years."

"Does Martin know?" Susan asked.

"Not yet. I must be very careful. He checks every piece of mail that comes and keeps tabs on my movements."

"So, how are you accomplishing your financial independence?"

"With Sally's help. She's noticed things change over the years and has been supportive of me. But, I can't go live with her. Martin thinks she's the best daughter in the world and I don't want her to have to face his anger for protecting me."

"How can we help you?"

"Just be on call. My attorney has contact with the women's shelter. She says the paperwork should be finished in a few days. I'll call you then and arrange a meeting place. I'll need to leave the area quickly without a trace."

"I understand. We'll drive you wherever you want to go. Remember, you're a Tiger."

"Thanks. That's what gave me courage to call. I have to go now. Martin may roll over and notice I'm not in bed and come looking for me. I'll call as soon as I can."

Susan tossed and turned the rest of the night, imagining what must be happening at Tiger's house to make her too afraid to ask Martin for a divorce. *"Oh, yes,"* she remembered, *"he would cut off all access to any joint funds, that is, if he even agreed to the divorce."*

About 6 a.m., Susan, tired of all those thoughts about Mary Ellen's crisis and her own memories running around in her brain, crawled out of bed and took a quick shower to try to clear her mind. Soon the coffee pot was emitting an aroma that was sure to awaken the soundest sleeper. Elise staggered out of the guest room, and sounding worshipful, she said, "Coffee, the nectar of the gods! Thank you." At the same time, Robin emerged and began to head for the bathroom.

"You look tired. Didn't you sleep well?" Susan asked Elise.

"Not really. Robin and I talked a long time about the situation and couldn't come up with any good ideas. Finally, sleep ambushed us, and we drifted off. I don't know about her, but I had weird dreams all night. You don't look wide awake either. How was your night?"

"I slept, but restlessly until 2:00 am when Tiger called."

Robin walked into the kitchen looking like she'd dunked her head in the basin to wake up. The hair around her face was damp. "Did you say Tiger called? What did she say?"

Susan recounted her middle-of-the-night conversation, ending with Mary Ellen's request for them to be on call for a few days while she worked out legal details.

"I can't do that," Elise said, "I told my husband I'd be home tomorrow."

"Nor I," Robin added. "I only took two days off work."

As they sat around the dining table sipping coffee and munching on bagels, Robin said, "We have to go home. That's firm, but what if we give you some money to help with Tiger's get away? I can write a check for $500."

Elise chimed in, "Great idea. I can add another $500. If we do that, can you handle the logistics?"

"That should work. Your $1,000 and my connections here should be adequate to get her someplace safe. She said she's trying to secure a financial agreement that he can't break. So, she should be good once she's settled somewhere away from here."

"That's our plan then," Robin said. "We'll get showered and head out to do some tourist things. I told my husband we were doing a girls' mini-vacation, so I have to go home with photos and souvenirs."

"Do you have to cover up your actions, too? Will we need to rescue you?"

"No. Bob is a good husband. He just doesn't think people should get mixed up in other people's business, especially married people."

With a plan decided, the three set off to visit the historic triangle sites of Jamestown Settlement, Colonial Williamsburg and the American Revolution Museum at Yorktown. By visiting the sites in that order, they covered the span of time from when the first English settlers arrived in 1607 to the last major battle of the American Revolution in 1782.

The next morning, after a filling breakfast of eggs, hash browns and fruit, Susan drove Robin and Elise to the airport. On the way home, she stopped at her bank and cashed their checks, taking the money in $100 bills.

***

After her brief call to Susan, Mary Ellen retreated to the bathroom and drew herself a tub of hot water and added some tea tree oil to ease her soreness and bruising. It was obvious that Martin no longer considered her a romantic partner. Foreplay and gentleness had long since disappeared from their relationship and been replaced by actions that at times indicated a need to release frustration and at other times demonstrated a need to dominate and punish. She never asked why. She learned that lesson when she asked Martin why he hit her. He responded something like, "It's your own fault. You didn't cook my eggs the way I like them." The change in him had taken place over the past few years. Or had it?

Thinking back, Mary Ellen recalled several incidents earlier when Martin had used threats of violence to keep her obedient. He acted like it was a joke, but Mary Ellen sensed the level of potential danger underlying his words. In the early days, his actions weren't violent, but insistent and insensitive, such as demanding sex at inappropriate times, like when she was ill or had just given birth. Sometimes, when they had guests, he would rise from his chair, take her hand and say, "I need some relaxation before I go to sleep." When those same guests declined a second invitation to their house, Martin accused Mary Ellen of being a poor hostess. But despite that bad behavior, there were enough good times that she dismissed those incidents and filed the behavior in a "But, he's a good dad and provides for us" category.

The violence problem did not become confined only to her. Martin beat the kids for minor infractions. He called it "spanking," but their bruises revealed what it really was. She remembered the time when she had to put bandages on their son's legs. She prayed that he would not get injured at school and the nurse would have to pull his pants off to dress the wound. Now, she thought that discovery might have been a good thing. But at the time, all she could think of was that if discovered, the nurse would have called the military police and then Martin would have been reduced in rank. Their budget was tight enough as it was.

On some occasions, he would punish the kids by making them stand with their arms extended, balancing books on their hands. She had to take responsibility for that particular method of punishment. Once, Martin and Mary Ellen were talking about their own childhoods, and Mary Ellen mentioned that one of her middle-school teachers used to punish students that way. Martin thought that was a good idea, and he immediately added it to his discipline repertoire. But the weight of the books was too much for their small bodies.

Why had she stayed so long and put the kids and herself through such pain? Fear was the main factor. Mary Ellen didn't think she could support herself and the kids on whatever job she might be able to land. Sometimes they were at overseas locations, so she couldn't leave without Martin authorizing travel back to the U.S.

All these memories were replays of incidents that had circled through her brain many times. Martin never admitted that he had a problem; rather, he told her that she did. Mary Ellen's eyes became open to Martin's psychological abuse in the Al-Anon group's meetings which she had been secretly attending for six months. She attended daytime meetings at a church close enough to walk to. Once she found the courage to speak up, she poured out her regrets, blaming herself for what had happened. "I should have …." "If only I would have…." "Perhaps I could have…." Each time the other women had assured her that living in a "shoulda, woulda, coulda" frame of mind would not solve anything. She needed to tell herself that she had done the best that she could do with the information she had at the time. After a few weeks passed, she mentioned that she no longer had to protect the children, so she could leave. After that meeting, one of the women handed her a list of community resources and suggested she call for help.

She called, and a caring woman guided her through the process of applying to receive a portion of Martin's retirement benefit. It wasn't a lot, but if she lived modestly and found a part-time job, she'd be fine. The paper work was almost finished without Martin's knowledge. He would be summoned to court to sign the papers within the week. She must be ready to depart directly from that meeting.

***

With her resolve set and her body aches somewhat soothed, Mary Ellen toweled off and returned to bed. Her weight settling on the mattress roused Martin. "Oh, you smell good, baby." He began to touch her breasts. The touching turned to squeezing, and her body stiffened.

She whispered, "Please not now. We both have to get up soon."

"But you smell good, and we're awake anyway."

"I'm still sore from earlier. Can't we wait until tomorrow night?"

"Are you refusing me?"

"No, just asking for a delay until my soreness eases."

"You always put your wants ahead of my needs," he told her as he lifted himself above her.

"Ow!" Mary Ellen screamed in pain.

"Stop pretending. You know you like it rough."

Knowing resistance was futile, Mary Ellen stopped protesting. She hated submitting to him, but her inner tiger reminded her that these middle-of-the night-invasions would be ending soon.

***

Two days later, Mary Ellen's phone rang. It was the shelter's advisor reporting that their attorney had drawn up the support papers after working closely with a military finance specialist who knew exactly what she would be able to receive. The advisor said that she would contact Martin to schedule a signing meeting and that the military advisor would be there. She suggested that Mary Ellen pack a bag and spend the next few nights at the shelter so that Martin would not be able to retaliate physically. Mary Ellen then called Susan and explained what was happening and explained that she would need to leave the area as soon as Martin signed the papers.

***

What Mary Ellen didn't know was that Martin had turned his suspicions about Susan, Elise and Robin's visit into an investigation. He hired a private detective who put a wiretap on their home phone and listened to the conversation about the shelter meeting and subsequent departure plans.

When he reported this information to Martin, the two of them planned how to thwart the escape effort. The investigator asserted that he was an advisor only and would not participate in any actions taken against Mary Ellen or the other women. He would not do anything that might jeopardize his detective license. He reported that the meeting would be at a neutral location, probably the courthouse, because the shelter would not allow an "alleged abuser" anywhere near their facility. That meant there would be less protection. Even so, Martin had to be careful not to take any overt actions when witnesses were present. "If you harm her, man, you're on your own. If police are involved, I will say that I advised you to allow her to leave and to comply with any court-ordered support payments."

***

Mary Ellen awoke in the women's shelter two days later. As she showered and prepared for the confrontation, she wondered how her marriage had deteriorated into this frightening situation. *Why hadn't she taken action years ago? Why had she made her children suffer too? Would Martin sign the papers and let her go? What has he been doing to prepare for or prevent this separation? Still, I'm grateful that I don't have broken bones, burns and knife wounds like some of the others here.*

Remembering that every reading taught her how to take care of herself, she picked up her Al-Anon daily reader and studied the message for that day. Being new to the program, Mary Ellen was still amazed that each day's inspiration seemed to fit what was happening that day. That day's message reminded her to trust herself and God for everyone's highest good.

After breakfast with the other women in the shelter, she rode with her attorney to the Hampton courthouse where everyone would meet to sign the petition for divorce and assignment of financial support. She had confirmed that a military attorney, who would be able to define Mary Ellen's rights as a military spouse, would be there. As they travelled, the women reviewed what would happen and what might happen. Mary Ellen reported, "Susan will meet us at the courthouse and park in the adjoining lot for a quick departure after the hearing. I'm eager to start a new life, yet apprehensive about Martin's behavior and my ability to support myself." The advocate assured her, "You are stronger than you think. You survived all these years with Martin. Living alone will be easy in comparison."

Meanwhile, Susan was making her own preparations. She had a small overnight bag packed, a computer map showing directions to Baltimore and the $1,000 that Elise and Robin had given to help Mary Ellen. The women thought Baltimore would be close enough for Mary Ellen to return for the divorce hearing and not a likely place Martin would look for her. They assumed he would look for her in the immediate area or at her brother's house.

Martin was at the courthouse, meeting with his own attorney, whom he had told that the split was amicable, but he really wanted to save the marriage. The lawyer said he'd do what he could to persuade the judge that reconciliation was possible. As Mary Ellen and her advocate arrived, Martin's attorney turned to him in surprise. "I know that woman. She handles pro bono cases from the women's shelter. Are you being truthful with me? I can't defend a client who has not given me the actual facts."

Martin assured the attorney, "I told you the truth. Mary Ellen must have selected her from the phone book, thinking she'd be more sympathetic because she's female." The men walked toward the hearing room with grim faces.

The judge, a middle-aged man who appeared to be chronically stressed, called the hearing to order. He requested the petitioner to speak first. Mary Ellen's advocate stepped forward and asked permission to speak for the client. The judge agreed with the stipulation that he might call her client later. The shelter attorney related, "On Tuesday, Mary Ellen Schuman arrived at the shelter by bus with just a small overnight bag. Because of our earlier discussion, I drove her to a physician, who has a contract with the shelter, for an examination. The doctor found traces of a bruise remaining around Mary Ellen's eye, more recent bruising on her upper arms and significant genital damage. Here's a copy of her report."

The judge frowned as he read the report, then asked what recompense they were seeking. The advocate responded, "We are asking you to rule that Mr. Schuman is allowed no contact with our client and that he provide a monthly stipend of $1,000. This amount has been approved by the Judge Advocate General's office at Fort Eustis." She then introduced the military attorney.

The judge called the military attorney forward and asked if the amount had been approved by the finance office. "Yes, sir. this amount has been approved after a review of Mr. Schuman's retirement pay and his current employment benefits."

"Thank you, Captain. Will Mr. Schuman's attorney step forward?"

Martin's attorney stepped forward, saying, "Your honor, I decline to represent Mr. Schuman. He was not forthcoming with these details when I agreed to take this case. When we saw Ms. Brown outside, I asked him if he had told me all the facts. He responded that he had been truthful in our discussions."

"Your statement is noted. Mr. Schuman, I rule that you will pay $1,000 per month to this court. That money will be forwarded to Mrs. Schuman. You are to have no further contact with her. This court will set a divorce hearing date and notify both parties who will be expected to appear or face penalties."

Martin stormed out of the courtroom, but he stopped just outside the building doors. As the women passed, he yelled at Susan and the advocate. "All this is your fault! You put her up to this and all of you will pay!" Fortunately for the women, the tirade was witnessed by a deputy, who promptly arrested Martin for intimidating a witness and led him to the jail.

As the three women walked to the parking lot, the shelter's attorney advised Mary Ellen, "Please don't think this arrest will stop Martin's behavior. His stint behind bars will just give him time to plot more violence. I suggest you continue your plans to escape this area and start a new life. Please provide your new address to Susan and to me. I can represent you at the divorce hearing, too."

Climbing into her car, Susan asked Mary Ellen, "Is there anything else you'd like to get from your house before we head to Baltimore? Since Martin is temporarily in jail, we have time to pick up a few things." Mary Ellen needed to retrieve some items, and she gave Susan directions to her home. When they arrived, she grabbed a couple photos of her children off the living room wall and then ran into the bedroom to gather more clothes. As Mary Ellen gathered, Susan carried the clothes, toiletries and photos out to her car. She also grabbed the coffee pot, a few pans, utensils and dishes. As Susan worked, she hollered into the bedroom, "Remember to grab a few towels and a set of sheets. You'll need that $1,000 for a place to stay."

By nightfall, Mary Ellen was tucked into a Baltimore women's shelter. Her advocate had called to let them know she was coming. The plan was that Mary Ellen could stay there while she looked for work and found an apartment. They had a list of places that offered temporary work with a certain amount of safety. Susan registered at a local motel. She planned to check on Mary Ellen in the morning then return to her home in Williamsburg. She had told her next-door neighbor that she would be out of town for a few days and asked her to call the police if she noticed any suspicious activity.

The next morning transpired as both the women anticipated. The Baltimore shelter had called Hampton to confirm Mary Ellen's arrival. They then announced that, starting the next morning, she would be working at the local Goodwill Store sorting donated items that would be priced and placed in the display area. She would be working in the storage area and have no reason to go onto the sales floor, not that they expected Martin to discover her whereabouts. But, even so, a little precaution could save a lot of hurt, Mary Ellen thought. In the meantime, a shelter advocate would go with her to find a suitable apartment convenient to the bus line that passed by the Goodwill Store.

Within a few days Mary Ellen settled into her routine. As she moved into her efficiency apartment, she sent a silent "thank you" to Susan for remembering to pack those household items. She called her children and told them that she was "out of town" until the divorce was settled. They promised not to tell their father that she had called. The shelter advocate had cautioned her not to tell them her location, because his entreaties might overshadow their loyalty to her.

***

In the meantime, Martin was getting angrier by the day. *How could the judge make such a ruling - $1,000 a month support! Outrageous! What had he done to deserve this treatment?* He called the military finance office to cancel the deduction and was told that they were legally bound to comply. The Finance Officer added that he still had his work salary to supplement his remaining retirement benefit and one less person to feed. He should be able to make ends meet without problem.

As the days passed, Martin drank more and more. No matter how much he drank, the booze did not diminish his anger. The drinking was also beginning to affect his job performance. He was called into Employee Assistance for guidance. They told him that he was on probation. He had to stop drinking, attend AA meetings, come to work on time every day and adequately perform his job duties. Any slip-ups would result in instant termination. This time Martin was too humiliated to shout. Doing a good day's work for a decent day's pay had always been his motto. His dad lived by this code, as had his grandfather. He could not shame his family name.

After leaving work, Martin drove to a nearby AA clubhouse to attend a meeting. He was welcomed warmly, given a cup of coffee and told to have a seat. The meeting started with someone reading the 12 Steps and 12 traditions. As the other participants began to share, Martin began to think: *I don't need to be there. I've never been to jail, except for those few hours after the separation hearing. I've never been institutionalized, and I still have my job – for now.*

Soon a man in suit pants and a dress shirt began to speak. "Hi, my name is Jim. I thought a few drinks would help solve my family problems. Soon, I was drinking on the job and put on probation. They told me I had 30 days to sober up or lose my job." Martin felt like the man was looking at him with every word. *How dare he single me out for his lecture?* He wanted to get up to leave but the Employee Assistance person was adamant in his instructions. *I guess I have to stay and listen to this crap.* Martin continued sipping his coffee and wishing he'd poured a stiffener in it. When he was invited to share, Martin declined.

Finally, the meeting ended, and not a minute too soon. Martin had no idea an hour lasted that long. Jim, the man who had spoken last, approached Martin and said, "You appear to be where I was five years ago. Want to talk about it?"

"You have to come here for five years?"

"As long as it takes. I found sobriety after a few meetings, but I continued to attend to learn how to stay sober. Now I come to give back a little of what was given to me. You know that Bill W. and Dr. Bob were hopeless drunks before they started this program. Now look how many people rely on their teachings."

"Who are Bill W. and Dr. Bob?"

"Dr. Bob and Bill were the founders of this program. Through trial and error, they found that sharing their problems helped them stay sober. Would you be willing to tell me what brought you here?"

Martin nodded, and Jim directed him to have a seat and brought coffee refills. "Okay, what brought you here?"

Martin slowly began telling about his meeting with Employee Assistance. Jim then asked what led up to that meeting.

"My wife. She went to court and told the judge all sorts of lies about me."

"The judge believed that without hearing your side?"

"Well, her attorney, a female, claimed she had a doctor's report listing all these terrible things I supposedly did. She said my wife had bruises and internal damage that I caused. That's a lie! I just expected her to do her job as a wife."

"And, those duties involved being injured by you?" Jim continued to ask questions gently until Martin revealed that he had "hit her a couple times" and "expected her to keep me happy, if you know what I mean."

Jim said he understood and suggested that Martin attend meetings every day for a while. "Here's my phone number. I'm willing to be your temporary sponsor, if that's okay with you?"

"What's a sponsor?"

"That's a person you call every day in the beginning when you want a drink or have a problem that bothers you."

"Call every day? The EA people told me I had to attend a meeting every day. And go to work. You expect me to do all that? I won't have time for anything else."

Jim chuckled, "That's the idea. We keep you so busy thinking about sobriety that you don't have time to wander into a bar."

Martin, feeling overwhelmed, asked, "This will keep me from drinking?"

"Well, we have a saying in AA, 'It works if you work it.' In other words, if you concentrate on staying sober instead of your problems, you will stay away from your favorite anesthetic."

"Anesthetic, huh? I guess that's about right. I drink to dull the pain."

***

For a few months, Mary Ellen went to work every day and actually enjoyed sorting the donations. Those tasks gave her something to think about instead of what might happen when the court set the divorce hearing date and she'd have to face Martin again. Soon the Goodwill administrators noticed how efficiently she worked and how well she got along with her co-workers. They also noticed that she had a knack for helping them solve problems without seeming to tell them what to do. She would listen to their woes and then say something like, "What would happen if you tried this or that?" That skill earned her a promotion to lead worker. Once she felt comfortable as lead worker, Mary Ellen began to read about Goodwill's business model and how they managed to help so many people when it appeared their income was donated clothes and goods that they sold at bargain basement prices. At the same time, they gave food to people in need.

During her off hours, she spent most of her time in her tiny apartment. She had found a library nearby and was catching up on some of the classics which she hadn't read since high school or which were on her long "to read" list. A couple of times she adventured into a nearby park for a long walk. She was feeling confident that Martin couldn't find her in this large city, but the fear never quite left. She also found an Al-Anon group that met in a church just two blocks away. There she found friends who supported her adventure of living in a new city. Even so, she didn't feel safe enough to tell them that she was being hidden from her abusive husband.

***

One day, an envelope arrived with the Hampton courthouse's return address in the upper left corner. Mary Ellen eagerly tore it open to find that a divorce date had been set and that she was ordered to appear. *Thank God! This will all be over soon, and I can live a normal life again!* As she scanned the letter, her relief turned to terror. The person typing the order had included Martin's home address and hers too! He would receive this same letter and know where she was!

In panic, she ran into the house and called her Al-Anon sponsor. The woman managed to comprehend most of what Mary Ellen was relating through her tears. She said, "I'll be right there to pick you up. You can stay at my house until you go to court. Do you have someone who will take you there?"

"Yes," Mary Ellen whispered. The woman's gentle words and assurance calmed her enough that she was able to begin thinking clearly again. "Susan, the woman who brought me to Baltimore, told me to call her when the date was set, and she would drive me back to Hampton."

"Have you talked to her in all these months?"

"Yes, she told me to call her each Sunday afternoon, and if she wasn't there, just to leave a message about how I was. She's been there most Sundays, just missing a couple when she had family obligations. She always told me when those would be occurring, so I wouldn't worry."

By this time, Mary Ellen was feeling more relaxed and told her sponsor that she would be fine in her security building.

***

As the weeks passed, Martin continued attending meetings and talking to Jim on a regular basis. Work was going much better. At one meeting he said, "Maybe I was a little critical of my wife, but I still resent her leaving. Why didn't she just say she was going? I would have tried to talk her out of it, but she had no reason to be afraid." Jim responded, "One day at a time. Don't dwell on the past or try to imagine the future."

After the meeting, Jim told Martin to grab another cup coffee and have a seat, because they had some things to discuss. They refilled their cups and sat down in the now empty meeting room. "Martin, you are making progress in your assessment of your relationship, but I don't see you accepting your share of the responsibility for the court order. Part of this is my fault. I haven't pushed you do write out your 4th Step and do the 5th step with me: 'Admitted to God, to ourselves and to another human being the exact nature of our wrongs.' What do you have to say about that?"

"Why should I do Step 5, when I can't do the 9th, "Made direct amends…?'"

"At least you've learned the steps. That's a start. Let's get back to Steps 4 and 5. I want you to start writing tonight. We'll meet before tomorrow's meeting to discuss your progress."

Grudgingly, Martin agreed and went home to write his 4th Step: "Made a searching and fearless inventory of ourselves."

What he wrote was:

"Was a bit grouchy from time to time.

"Hit Mary Ellen a few times, but she deserved it.

"Was pretty strict with the kids, but they earned each punishment.

"Generously paid for their college tuition and watched all their stupid school events, even though I didn't want to.

"Gave them all a comfortable home to live in.

"Missed them when I was in Iraq and wrote once a week. Sometimes I forgot.

"Drove them everywhere they wanted to go, even when I wanted to watch the big game on television."

***

When the two of them met at the club house the next afternoon after work, Jim read the list, took a long, deep drink of coffee and excused himself to use the bathroom. *How am I going to challenge Martin's list of justifications for his behavior and keep him coming to meetings? I don't want to send him back to the bottle. If that happens, he'll lose his job and will probably go deeper into the disease.* After thinking a few minutes and washing his hands, Jim remembered, *I was almost that useless when I first came to the program. What did my first sponsor tell me? Oh, I remember. Will it work? Well, it worked for me.*

Returning to the table, Jim told Martin to look him in the eye. He took a deep breath and said, "Martin, this list is pure bullshit. Go home and do it over again. We'll meet here tomorrow and every day until you see your part in your problems and why you drink."

After three tries, Martin finally made a list to which Jim reluctantly accepted with the caveat, "I want you to do this again in three months, just to check on your progress."

***

As time went by at work, Mary Ellen developed efficient techniques for sorting the donations. She loved working and chatting with her co-workers. They had seen enough cases like hers. In fact, a couple were in similar situations. So, when she said that she was separated and offered no further details, no one asked prying questions. Mary Ellen's tasks and new friends gave her something to think about instead of what might happen when she'd have to face Martin again at the divorce hearing.

At the Al-Anon group, Mary Ellen did her 4th and 5th step, listing such items as not protecting the children well enough, not providing better meals for Martin and complaining when he hit her. Her sponsor said, "This list reads like you are still taking responsibility for Martin's actions. You need to do it over again, remembering what you did right as well as those things that promoted disharmony. Remember, taking inventory also means listing those things you did well. You told me you received a promotion at work. Apparently, someone appreciates you."

***

As he arrived home that same day, Martin found an official looking envelope in his mailbox. He opened it and found that a date had been set for the divorce hearing. The letter suggested that if he didn't have an attorney, he should find one to represent him. *Damn! She really went through with it! Oh, here's her address. She lives in Baltimore. Damn! I could have seen her and didn't even know it. I need to talk to her right away. If I tell her I've been attending AA meetings and passed my work probation, she'll come back, and we can forget all this divorce nonsense.*

Calling his AA sponsor, Martin relayed the information and told Jim that he was going to drive up to Baltimore to try to persuade her to drop the divorce petition. Jim suggested, "There's a meeting at 8 p.m. at the Baptist Church. You have plenty of time to have supper and calm down before you go."

"I don't need to calm down. I need to talk to my wife and settle all this nonsense."

"It's not nonsense. Remember you have a court order to stay away from her until the hearing."

"That court order is just for Hampton. She lives in Baltimore. It was on the court papers."

"Are you sure about that? I think the order is good for anywhere in the U.S. Let's go grab something to eat before the meeting."

"Not tonight. I need to talk to Mary Ellen before the court date and tell her how I've changed."

"You've just recently come off probation at work, but you're still skating on thin ice with your supervisor. If I were you, I wouldn't jeopardize my job again."

"I have to do this. I'll talk to you when I get back."

***

After re-reading the court summons, Mary Ellen called Susan. "Good news! The hearing is in two weeks. I have to appear in person."

Susan responded, "Wonderful! I'll drive up tomorrow. We can have lunch and plan the trip back to Williamsburg. You'll stay with me, unless you want to stay at the shelter, of course, for the time you have to be down here to sign papers and arrange whatever else needs to be resolved. I'm sure you'll want to get a few more things from your house."

"That's true. I want some of the kid's art work from school and my craft supplies. I've picked up a few small, self-contained projects from the craft store to fill my time and decorate my apartment. I hope Martin will let me in the house to retrieve them."

"I think the judge will order Martin to allow you access to the house to collect your personal belongings. The kids may have already taken what they want to keep. We'll find out when we get to court."

"Thank you, Susan. I'll check with the store manager tomorrow about taking off a couple days to handle this mess. I know she'll approve my leave. She came up through the ranks the hard way too, so she has been cheering me on while protecting my privacy."

"Okay, I'll meet you at the store about noon so that we can have lunch. Let me know what she says and when I need to be there to pick you up. G'bye."

After ending the call, Susan called Robin and Elise to give them the good news. They said they would fly in to support Mary Ellen at the divorce hearing.

***

After the phone call to Jim, Martin jumped into his car and began driving to Baltimore. He didn't even take time to eat supper, though he did remember to fill his gas tank and purchase two six-packs of Budweiser and a bottle of Jack Daniels. He drank six cans of beer as he drove up I-64. The sun was just setting, causing reflections and shadows. As he approached the merge onto I-95 near Richmond, he popped open another Bud. His GPS said this was the most efficient way to get to Baltimore. *Once I reach her house, I'll talk to her. Surely, after all this time, she will remember the good times and be willing to talk with me. She has little reason to be angry. I only hit her a few times and that was because she made me so mad.*

Martin took a deep swallow of the Bud as he merged onto I-95. He didn't see the pick-up truck in his blind spot. The truck knocked his car into the next lane where a grocery truck struck it, knocking his car into the guard rail and destroying it. The grocery trucker pulled over and immediately jumped out of his rig to post flares around the mess.

The pick-up driver pulled onto the emergency lane and stopped with his flashers blinking. He ran to check on the car's driver and found Martin slumped over the wheel with blood running down his face and onto the air bag that should have protected him from major injury. He called 911 and was told that emergency vehicles were already on the way. A passing driver who was unable to stop because of the traffic flow had already called. The 911 operator told him not to touch the injured man, because he might have an internal injury. Moving him could cause further damage.

He then checked on the tractor-trailer driver who had minor bruises, as he did, and for the first time he noticed that he had blood running down his leg. In the commotion, the pickup driver had not felt pain and hadn't thought to check his own body. The tractor-trailer trucker said, "I also radioed the police and my company. They told me to take photos and get checked at the hospital even though I don't feel injured. They'll send a representative to handle legal issues and assess damage to all three vehicles. That person will not arrive until tomorrow. In the meantime, I'm to follow whatever instructions the police give me."

By this time emergency vehicles were arriving. The EMTs saw that both truck drivers were on their feet, so they ran to the car crunched up against the guard rail. They popped the driver's side door open. The lead responder checked for Martin's pulse. There was none. She pulled out a stethoscope and listened for a heartbeat. Nothing. At that point, she waved the other EMTs to carefully lift Martin out of the car and onto the gurney. She checked him again for a heartbeat, and, finding none, she told them that it appeared he had died in the collision and to take him to the emergency room for a more thorough examination.

The EMT then turned her attention to the pick-up driver's bloody leg. She cleaned and bandaged the wound. "You're lucky this is the only injury you have. When you get home, have your doctor look at this. He'll probably want to put in a couple stitches and do a more thorough examination. Your BP and heart rate are close to normal. That's good for this situation." She then turned her attention to the tractor-trailer driver who appeared to be in good shape. She also suggested that he see his doctor to assure there were no unnoticed injuries. He responded that his company had already told him to do so.

In the meantime, the police noticed seven open Bud cans, spilled liquid and a broken Jack Daniels bottle on the car's floor and noted "suspected drunk driver" on their report. The toxicology report would confirm or deny their suspicions. They released the car to a tow-truck driver with instructions to deliver it to the police compound area for further inspection. At the hospital, the ER duty physician confirmed the EMT's conclusion and checked for identification. Finding Martin's driver's license, insurance card, a few credit cards and a cell phone, she turned these over to the police to find and notify next-of-kin.

Going through the phone's directory, the officer noticed that the most frequent calls were to a man named Jim. She called that number, identified herself and asked, "What is your relationship to Martin."

"I'm Martin's AA sponsor. If he was arrested for drunk driving, I will not bail him out. I'll check on him tomorrow after he's slept it off."

The officer took a deep breath and explained, "Martin has been in a car accident with suspicion of drunk driving. Can you provide the names and addresses of Martin's relatives?"

Jim paused as he guessed what that question foretold. He told her about his last conversation with Martin. She thanked him for his time, and then she went down to the impound lot to search for the letter with Mary Ellen's address. She found it up against the rear window where it had probably been thrown by the impact. She returned to the precinct, reported to her commander and then walked to her desk to call the Baltimore police.

***

Mary Ellen was eating her supper, home-made refried beans and rice with a few vegetables on the side and watching the tiny television she had bought at the Goodwill Store where she worked. Fortunately, her apartment complex provided basic cable so that she was able to watch a few local stations. She missed the big selection of channels available when she lived with Martin, but she was happy to do without because she now had peace of mind. Even so, fearful thoughts popped into her mind. *Martin might show up here since he now has my address. But, I'll be here in this secure building or at work. People will look out for me. The divorce hearing itself will be fine, because Susan will be there and also my shelter advocate. She was able to connect with an attorney who has a partnership agreement with the shelter to provide pro bono help for their clients. Oh, yes, police will be roaming the building, because the courthouse and police department are in the same building. If Martin creates a scene like at our earlier hearing, he'll go back to jail again.* At that, she smiled with relief.

Someone knocked on her door, probably her next-door neighbor. No one else could get in without buzzing her. Calling out, "Just a minute," Mary Ellen set her plate on the kitchenette counter and walked barefooted to the door. Seeing the police officer, she stepped back in shock. *What could she want? She'd been a good employee at Goodwill. Her children didn't even know where she was. Even Susan only had her phone number.*

"Mrs. Schuman?"

"Yes. May I help you?"

"I'm sorry, but I'm here to deliver bad news."

"My kids? What happened?"

"As far as I know, they are fine, Mrs. Schuman. I'm here to notify you that your husband, Martin Shuman, was killed in a car crash near Richmond earlier this evening."

Mary Ellen's eyes misted immediately with shock, but she didn't cry as she asked, "Please tell me what happened."

The police officer explained, "His car was struck by a pick-up that bumped him in front of a grocery truck. That impact caused Martin's death. We suspect he had been drinking and driving. Tests will confirm if this is the case or not. Do you have someone to stay with you?"

Mary Ellen nodded and retrieved her phone and called her Al-Anon sponsor, who said she'd be over immediately. Assured that Mary Ellen would have someone to assist her, the officer said she'd be in touch as soon as she had more information and that Mary Ellen would probably need to go to Richmond to sign papers and make burial arrangements for Martin.

Thanking the officer, Mary Ellen closed the door. She sat still, thinking of her life with Martin. *It had been good for a few years, exploring new surroundings when they moved from post to post. Sally had been born while Martin was serving in Dessert Storm. Bobby had been born in the Lansdtuhl Army Hospital. Their last assignment had been Fort Eustis, and they had bought their first home in nearby Hampton. By then the kids were in college, and they were on their own again. Sadly, Martin's occasional drinking had become daily. What had caused that? He had not shown the symptoms of PTSD that so many of his contemporaries had suffered. Had she really failed the marriage as Martin had told her so many times?*

Catherine, her sponsor, arrived. Mary Ellen told her what the police offer said. After asking a few more questions, Catherine suggested that Mary Ellen stay with her overnight. She should first call Sally and Bobby to give them the news. Then she should call Susan who could help her get through what had to be done back in Virginia. Catherine began washing dishes and packing fresh fruits and vegetables.

"What are you doing?" Mary Ellen asked.

"You won't be back here for several days, if then," Catherine answered. "After all, you now own the Hampton house and may decide to stay there. Now, go make those calls."

Sally and Bobby were distressed but more worried about their mother who unexpectedly had to make all the tough decisions that must be made in a family crisis. They were well aware that their dad had made all important decisions. They told their mom that they would join her at the Hampton house as soon as they could make arrangements.

When she heard the news, Susan responded, "I'll still drive up to Baltimore tomorrow, but I will take you to your home instead of to lunch. That way, you'll have all the legal documents you need to make those big decisions."

Catherine then took the phone to give Susan directions to her house and thanked her for taking on this responsibility.

"It's the least I can do," Susan told Catherine. Mary Ellen would do the same for me."

***

By early evening the next day, the two women had reached Williamsburg. "I don't know about you, but I'm exhausted," Susan said. "You may be a tiger, but neither of us has slept. Let's stay at my house tonight. That way, we'll be rested when we get to your house and better able to make the decisions that need to be made. You'll need to rent a car, too, since you only owned one, and it's been destroyed."

"Thank you. I hadn't thought about needing a car. I've been walking or taking the bus everywhere all these months."

They carried Mary Ellen's suitcase into the house and changed into their pajamas. Susan made two cups of chamomile tea. As she handed a cup to Mary Ellen, she said, "We've been reminiscing about your travels as an Army wife all day. Drink this and go to sleep. In the morning we'll start discussing legal details and funeral plans."

***

After a breakfast of homemade granola and Greek yogurt, the two women headed down I-64 to Hampton. "Do you know if Martin had a will and where he kept it?"

"He had to make a will before he went to Iraq the first time. That would be with the Legal Affairs office."

"Do you know if he updated it after he retired?"

"No, he took care of all our business, paying all the bills. He said he didn't want me to worry about such things."

"Okay," she sighed. *There is no use being upset with Mary Ellen. She had a big enough job trying to stay alive to protect her children to argue about such details.* "We may need to hire an attorney to research this information. They can usually find information in places that aren't readily available to us. Do you know if Martin had an attorney other than the one who came to court with him at the support hearing? That man obviously was not familiar with you or the situation."

"No, I'd never seen him before. Let me think. Oh, I remember. He hired a man named Harrison to handle the closing when we bought our home about five years ago. I remember that because I wondered if he was related to the colonial Harrisons who had such an impact on the colony's growth and later produced two U.S. presidents."

"That's a good place to start. We'll call him and go through what documents we find at the house, check with Legal Affairs and visit the bank to learn if he had a safe deposit box and what kinds of accounts he held. We'll also call the shelter attorney."

"Who knew this would be so difficult?"

"I don't like to say this, but it wouldn't be this hard if he'd kept you informed about his financial dealings. There, it's said, and now we can move on. You weren't involved in the decision-making process so would not be expected to know this information. Oh, by the way, did you ever think about what you might do after the divorce was settled?"

"Yes. In fact, I've been putting about $50 in a savings account each month. I've been considering enrolling at the technical college to get an associate degree in business. You know, I really like working at Goodwill. I didn't think I would in the beginning, but, I like it well enough that I'd like to move up in the company to store manager."

"Or you could go to another company and make better money."

"That's a good idea too."

"Your dream will probably start to come true as soon as all the paperwork is settled. I'm sure Martin had at least a couple thousand dollars in the bank. That will pay for your associate degree. Are you going to move back into your house?"

"I probably will while we're getting all the details straightened out. Later, I don't know. I really like Baltimore. I've found a new 'me' there."

"You are bringing the new 'you' back to Hampton now."

"True, there's so much to think about. This decision can wait until we learn what my financial situation is."

***

Soon they arrived at the Hampton house that until recently had been Mary Ellen's home. Tiger was nervous, not knowing what to expect. Had Martin kept the house clean? She didn't think he knew how to do homemaking chores. He certainly never helped her. He only complained when something didn't suit him.

"Luckily, I still have the key. I almost threw it out, not expecting to ever return here. But, something, intuition I guess, made me keep it on my key ring."

A few newspapers were strewn on the porch, and the mailbox was stuffed mostly with sales ads. She'd go through it later to see if there was anything important. When the door swung open, the women saw a few newspapers scattered around the living room. Three opened utility bills and a dirty glass sat on the end table next to Martin's favorite chair along with the Big Book of AA and the television remote. The kitchen trash held a few crumpled boxes that had contained frozen meals. Two cups, a saucer and another glass sat in the sink.

"Not bad," Mary Ellen said. "I expected worse." They walked through the remaining rooms noting that their condition was about the same. A few dirty clothes in the hamper and a couple of towels tossed over the shower curtain bar were all they found. Even the bed was made, military corners, of course.

"Well, it looks like he knew how to keep house and do laundry after all. Let's start searching for documents. Did he have a home office?" Susan asked.

"Yes, he set up a little office in the basement with a computer, file cabinet and everything."

They descended the basement stairs and found a desk with papers on the top and a few wadded documents in the waste basket. "This is unusual. He always kept everything filed away. He was a neat freak about his papers. He said that the Army had drilled document organization into his brain."

"Well, this is a gift to us. We can see what he was working on and maybe learn something of value before we have to dig into the file cabinet and start making phone calls."

They began sorting the papers into stacks: utility bills, bank statements, work documents, legal papers and so on. Apparently, he didn't plan on her returning, since nothing had been filed since their support hearing. As they continued sorting and reading, they learned a lot. Martin had thousands of dollars in two banks and investments with two brokerage firms. Old bills were paid, and new ones were in a desktop sorter along with his checkbook. One letter showed that he had tried to counter-sue Mary Ellen for abandoning the family, but the attorney refused to take the case after he read the court transcripts about the support hearing.

Once this mess was organized and the women had made notations on a paper tablet, they searched drawers, only to find the usual general office supplies: pens, pencils, tablets, staples, paper clips, printer cartridges, printer paper and a packet of high grade gray stationery. "He must have used this good paper for business and legal correspondence," Susan commented.

They tried to open the file cabinet but found it locked. There was no key for it on the desk. "Do you have the key ring the police gave you?" Susan asked.

"It's in my purse upstairs. I'll go look."

Soon Mary Ellen returned to the basement with two Pepsi cans and a key ring in her hand. "This one key is smaller and looks different. Let's try it first." The lock clicked, and all four drawers popped open, each one full. The top drawer promised to be the jackpot. It held more bank statements and brokerage correspondence. Taped to the side of the drawer was a 3"x5" card with the words, "Old Point, Mercury" and a series of numbers.

Susan exclaimed, "You may have struck oil. This must refer to Old Point Bank on Mercury Boulevard, and I'll bet this is his pass code to a safe deposit box. We can try to access it. Shall we go now?"

"Sure, let's find out what's in there."

They gathered their purses and walked out to the car. "Is Mercury Blvd. to the right as we leave here?

"No, I walked to the left when I caught the bus to go shopping."

"Didn't you ever drive?"

"Yes, remember we took Driver's Ed together in high school."

"That's right! So, didn't you drive around here?"

"No, we always owned only one car, and Martin drove it to work. I took the bus if I needed to go anywhere in town. He always drove when we went to the commissary or exchange."

"That means you always went on Saturday when they were crowded."

"Yes, and he always complained about the crowds."

"Well, now you can drive wherever you want."

"My license expired years ago, and I'll be nervous in this city traffic."

"We can take care of that. Those bank statements indicate you will have enough money to buy a small car and take driver lessons again. I know instructors are available. I see their signs on top of cars all over the place. First, let's check out this mysterious account. Tomorrow we'll make a list and start visiting the other bank and brokerage houses. Once we know what he's actually stashed away, you can begin to make plans."

***

"I'm sorry, but I can't allow you access to Mr. Schuman's box," said the site manager, Mr. Johnson. "His directions say the box is to be opened by him only."

"But he's dead. He died in a car crash three days ago."

"That changes things. You are?"

"His wife. I just found a notation about this account while I was going through his papers to plan his funeral."

"That's different. I can allow you access once you produce his death certificate and your identification."

"Oh, where can I get that?"

"From the funeral director."

"Okay. I'll call Parklawn. His body is there. The director told me to call when I was ready to discuss funeral details. I was out of town and just returned this morning. It seemed important to look through his papers for insurance information first."

"You call him, and when you bring the documentation, you can access his box."

The two women walked back out to the car. They both dug through their purses, looking for the phone number that the Baltimore police had given them. When the police had asked Mary Ellen where to take the body, she said, "Parklawn" because she recalled seeing it from the bus when she ran errands. Susan found the number quickly because she had programmed it into her phone. She punched the number and handed the phone to Mary Ellen, who explained what she needed.

The woman who answered the phone suggested that Mary Ellen come in right away because she had to sign some papers and make funeral arrangements. When Mary Ellen and Susan arrived at the Armistead Avenue site, they were welcomed by the woman who introduced herself as Catherine Baker, the director. "Good morning, you are Mrs. Schuman, is that correct?"

"Yes, this is my friend, Susan Wilson, who is helping me make all these decisions."

"Welcome, Ms. Wilson. Will you both step into my office so we can discuss what needs to be done?"

After discussing the details about the way Martin had died and when, Mary Ellen chose cremation and a short service on Friday with visitation for two hours before the funeral at 2 p.m. That way his work associates could stop in during their lunch period if they were unable to attend the funeral.

***

After stopping at the grocery to pick up fresh fruit and vegetables and a small box of deli-made chocolate chip cookies, the two women returned to the house. Mary Ellen began making phone calls, first to Sally and Bobby, and then to Martin's employer, other relatives and friends while Susan prepared a bountiful salad for lunch.

Suddenly, the house phone rang. The sound seemed out of place because the two women were accustomed to cell phone ring tones. Mary Ellen had picked up a phone at the Baltimore Wal-Mart that allowed her to buy only the usage minutes that she needed. That way she was able to keep the cost minimal.

Picking up the receiver, Mary Ellen said, "Schuman Residence," as Martin had always insisted. She assumed that whoever was calling would expect that response.

"May I speak to Martin, please?"

"He's not here right now. May I take a message?"

"This is Jim, one of Martin's friends, and I've been trying to reach him on his cell phone, but he hasn't answered. The last time we talked he was upset. I haven't seen him since, so I'm checking if he's okay."

"Jim, this is Mary Ellen, Martin's wife. I'm sorry to tell you that Martin died in a car crash on Saturday. His funeral will be Friday at Parklawn. Could you spread the word to his AA friends?"

"So, you know he's been attending AA?"

"I found a Big Book next to his chair with your name in it, so I guessed that he'd been going and that you're his sponsor. I've been attending Al-Anon for several months, even before our separation."

"Your guess is correct. I talked to him when he had just found your address and was going to try to convince you to stop the divorce proceedings. Did you talk?"

"No, he only made it as far as the I-64/I-95 interchange. The police found several open beer cans in the car and a broken bottle of Jack Daniels."

"I'm not surprised. That often happens in stressful situations. Do you need groceries or anything?"

"I'm okay, but, umm, could I ask another favor? Would you be willing to attend the funeral? I'd like to meet you and thank you in person for helping Martin."

"I'd be honored, and I'll check with the others at the clubhouse. We'll be sure all is in order."

***

The next day, Mary Ellen and Susan returned to the funeral home and finished up all the paperwork and arrangements. Ms. Baker handed over the death certificates and some reading materials about the grief process.

Concluding all those details, the two drove back to Old Point Bank and asked for Mr. Johnson. "Good afternoon, Mrs. Schuman, were you able to get a death certificate?"

"Yes. Here it is."

"Good, here's the key to his box. You just walk into that security room, find the box that matches the key. You can pull the box out and examine the contents on the table in there. I'm sorry, Ms. Wilson, you'll need to wait out here."

"I understand," Susan said. "I'll be right over there in the waiting area."

Mary Ellen did as she was instructed. Opening the box, she saw their marriage license and children's birth certificates. That surprised her. She thought those documents were in a small portable safe in the house. *He must have moved them after our split. I wonder why?* Continuing to sift through the documents, she found a will and a small black box. Opening the box, she found five diamonds that looked to be about 4 carats each. She gasped and grabbed hold of the table to keep from fainting. *No wonder we were on such a tight budget all those years. He must have been buying these diamonds and investing all along. I wonder what made him choose to invest in diamonds. What else might he have hidden from me?* Once she was able to breathe a little better, Mary Ellen read the purchase certificates and learned that he had bought the diamonds, one at a time, many years before when the price was much lower.

She put the diamonds back in the lock box and returned it to its place in the vault. Taking a deep, calming breath to slow her pulse to normal, she picked up the documents and returned to Mr. Johnson's office and asked, "Can I transfer this box to my name? I want to leave a few items in safe keeping."

"Of course, I have the death certificate showing you are the widow and have seen your identification. Just let me pull up a transfer document for you to sign. As it popped up, he turned the computer screen so that she could read and confirm the details and sign the signature pad. He then printed out a copy for her records. He escorted her and Susan to the waiting room, saying he looked forward to doing business with her in the future, and offering to transfer her other accounts to his bank if she wished.

"I'll need to think about those kinds of decisions. Thank you so much for your assistance."

***

While Susan drove to Langley Credit Union where Martin had maintained the checking account, Mary Ellen read the will she had found. It was dated just after his retirement when the children were still in college. She found that she was the primary beneficiary with smaller portions going to Sally and Bobby.

"I wonder why he didn't change the will when I left," Mary Ellen commented. "Did he really think I'd be back after all that happened?"

"Most likely," Susan said, "Men like Martin don't see their mistakes. They believe that any problems are the other person's fault. He probably assumed you'd soon come to your senses and beg forgiveness. Don was like that. Fortunately, I left the second time he hit me."

"You were fortunate to get out early,' Mary Ellen said, "Why I didn't leave when he hit the kids, I don't know."

Susan responded, "Don't start with those recriminations again. Remember what you learned in Al-Anon. You did the best you could with the resources and information you had at the time."

As the afternoon progressed, Susan drove Mary Ellen to two more banks and two brokerage offices. She learned that Martin had been stashing money for many years, probably since they were first married. As they had moved from one assignment to another, Martin had transferred the funds to local banks. The brokerage accounts just moved from one branch to another. Mary Ellen completed paper work at each site to transfer the funds to her name. Since she had both the death certificates and the will, a consultant at each site helped here through the process.

"You are now a wealthy woman, my friend," Susan commented as they prepared supper together. Mary Ellen did the cooking while Susan set the table. "You seem to be handling this pretty well. Did you suspect he was stashing funds?"

"No, but today's findings clarified many questions about our financial situation. Our Army friends traveled around Europe and took vacations here in the U.S. We never had money to do those things. Martin said it was because the kids cost so much to keep in clothes and he had to save for their college tuition."

"Did he save for their tuition?"

"Yes, they earned some scholarships, but he paid the rest. Of course, there were no frills like semesters in Europe. They both have great jobs now. So, saving pennies all those years was worth it."

"Well, it looks like he was planning a comfortable retirement too. Don't forget that we need to go to the Fort Eustis Legal Affairs office tomorrow to learn what to do about the monthly support payments the court ordered and if you're entitled to widow's benefits."

In the morning they learned that Mary Ellen was entitled to a portion of Martin's retirement benefit and that it would start soon.

They also arranged for a military representative with a U.S. flag to be at the funeral and present it to her during the service.

The next day was Tuesday. Sally and Bobby arrived and stayed at the house with their mom. Since their arrival, Robin and Elise returned with Susan to her home each night. Other relatives arrived on Wednesday and Thursday and stayed at hotels. Mary Ellen insisted on feeding them all at her house. Only the children had known about the separation, and no one mentioned it now. Several guests commented about how stoic Mary Ellen was being about losing her beloved husband. Martin was such a loving father.

When possible, the children jumped into the conversation, "Mom was always one to keep her chin up in a crisis. Then she'd fall apart later. That will probably happen this time too. That's why we're staying here an extra week to get her through that tough time. We also have her minister and doctor on speed dial for quick assistance, should it be needed."

Bart took his sister aside and told her he was glad that Martin had provided for her future. "Truthfully, I didn't think he would. In my work I deal with people like him every day. I spotted his behavior-cover-up patterns years ago."

"Why didn't you say something?"

"Sis, you know you would have rejected my assessment and accuse me of trying to break up your marriage. I kept quiet so that when an emergency occurred like this, you'd trust me to help you."

"I guess you're right. I learned that much in Al-Anon. Thank you for being honest with me now. It's good to know that someone understands what I've been through. Did you know I've been in protection for the past few months?"

"I suspected it. Each time I called, Martin said you were "out" with no further explanation. It sounded like a cover-up to me. I knew the kids would call if things got really bad."

They hugged and returned to their family gathered around the snack table.

***

The time for the funeral arrived. Everyone – family, co-workers, AA/Al-Anon friends and a few neighbors - showed up. The minister had asked the family for some favorite memories. He delivered a moving eulogy that included memories of a caring husband and dad who proudly attended baseball games and band concerts. He then turned events over to an Army officer who presented a flag to Mary Ellen in honor of Martin's long and dedicated service to the United States. At that point, her tears began to fall. Even though he was a tough father and a cold husband, he was an honorable solder. He provided well and always made sure they had a nice place to live, whether on base or off. Now, he left her a wealthy woman. He must have loved her, even though his actions seemed to indicate that she was beneath regard.

***

Months passed. Mary Ellen returned to her job at Goodwill. Since she was no longer under a protection order, she began working in the sales end of the business and found she was good at it. She took driving lessons and bought a red Ford Fiesta. The investments and checking accounts stayed where they were, only now in her name. She moved to a larger apartment in a nicer building, though it was hard to say good-bye to the friends she'd made in the secure building where everyone looked out for each other.

When Susan or her family called, she told them about concerts she'd attended and museums she'd visited. They were pleased that she was now enjoying all the activities that had been limited during her time with Martin and unavailable during her protection period.

***

One sunny day, Mary Ellen pulled her still new car into the garage at her new apartment building. She walked upstairs to the lobby to check her mail. Opening the box, she found a phone bill, a letter from her sister and a large manila envelope. It was from Johns Hopkins University and said she had been accepted into the Business program in her chosen support area, Social Work. She hugged the envelope to her chest, smiling and dancing her way to the elevator.

Humor Section

A Halloween to Remember

It was 1968. Orville had recently returned from his second tour in Vietnam and had purchased a small house in Copperas Cove, Texas. A few local families were the backbone of the community. The rest of us were military families attached to Fort Hood.

To give you a little background: Orville grew up in rural West Virginia where Halloween costumes were whatever Mom could scrape together out of old clothes. Because they lived in the country, the kids only went trick-or-treating at two or three houses.

I grew up in an Ohio town that was large enough to have three elementary schools. Towns were safer then, so we older kids went in groups carrying shopping bags or pillow cases and had the run of neighborhoods that were within walking distance.

About a week before Halloween, Orville and I went commissary-shopping. I began piling bags of candy into the cart. He returned most of the candy to the shelves. I put it back in the cart. He asked, "Why are you buying so much candy?"

"For Trick-or-Treat."

"You're buying too much."

"No, I'm not. We need much more than this."

"How much candy do you plan to give each child?"

"Two pieces."

"Then one bag should be enough."

"No, it won't. The Smiths have four children. The Jones' have five. We have three. The rest of the families on our street have approximately the same number, and kids will be coming from other neighborhoods."

"You can't be serious."

"I am. We need at least 12 bags of candy. Twenty would be better."

"I don't think so, but I'll agree to 10 bags."

"That won't be enough."

"That's all I'm buying," Orville said, folding his arms.

On Halloween, I put the candy in a soup kettle and asked Orville to watch for Trick-or-Treaters while I dressed our three little ones in their homemade costumes. I reminded him not to give anyone more than two pieces.

"We'll have candy left for Easter," he complained.

"No, we won't. Remember, I grew up in town and know what kind of crowd to expect."

Soon, the doorbell rang and there stood four little beggars. Three more arrived just as Orville was handing candy to the first group. Then came another five. After that, there were Superman, a cowboy, a doctor, a princess and more. Orville ran to grab his movie camera and said, "You pass out the candy. I'm filming this."

"We agreed that I'd take the kids out and you'd pass out the candy," I said.

"We'll pay the neighbor girl a dollar to take the kids out. I have to get this on camera."

And so the evening went, until we were down to two bags of candy. I told Orville that I needed to make more treats and headed for the kitchen. I had baked cookies that day, just in case candy ran out. Two cookies went into each sandwich bag. Soon all our apples, oranges and bananas flew into outstretched treat bags. Then I began popping and bagging popcorn.

That was nearly gone when, finally, curfew hit, and we were able to take a few deep breaths. Orville said, "I can hardly believe what I just saw. Next year we'll be better prepared."

I couldn't resist tossing a "told you so" in his direction.

The following year, not only did we buy more candy, but Orville also invited another couple to bring their candy to our house. The men passed out the candy and filmed the Trick or Treaters while we moms took our preschoolers house-to-house, then returned to make sure the snacks kept coming. We had to pop corn again.

A Mini-Con-Man

How early does a kid learn to con adults? I think he learns it in the crib. (I'm using a boy in my example because that is what my great-grands are. Girls are equally conniving.)

If I cry, Mommy or Daddy will come and hold me. If Grandma is here, she'll try to beat my parents to the crib. I love watching them all try to come through in the doorway at the same time. That's so funny, but I keep crying until one of them picks me up.

Then the little darling turns two. He soon learns to sit on the potty chair without filling said chair until Mom, Dad or Grandma gets tired of reading stories. Then, exactly one minute after the pull-up is back in place, the tot fills it. The adult gets frustrated and turns red in the face but won't yell because the little angel tried. Then he gets more attention while getting his pull-up changed.

As he starts pre-school, he learns even more conniving tricks from his classmates, such as, "I *really, really, really* want it," while making the irresistibly sad little face. So, the adult, especially Great-grandma, gives in, and the little sweetie receives his new toy.

As the child progresses through pre-school and kindergarten, his approach becomes subtler and powerfully effective: He strikes just the right posture, admiring the toy with wide eyes which he turns to you, and he proclaims, "I don't need a new toy. I just want to look at it."

Try to say no to that!

As kindergarten ends, the little sweetie can read simple words. He asks Great-grandma to take him to "the library that sells toys," i.e., Barnes and Noble. He runs straight to the toy department, carefully not noticing a single book, even those on special display. Finally, Great-grandma steers him to the train play table with several of the "Thomas the Tank Engine" family members just sitting there, waiting to be joined together and driven around the tracks, over bridges and into the round house.

After playing quietly and sharing the trains with other little boys for about an hour, the child notices, as if he had not seen them until that moment, the train cars sitting on the sales display. He points out several new double-car sets. Great-grandma explains that they cost too much. The boy scans the display and names aloud the train cars that he already had. Then he comes to the one named Patrick. "This one is Patrick. I don't have him."

"Maybe you'll get one for Christmas."

"But, Patrick is my little brother, and I love him."

No need to describe how this story ended.

A New WMD (Weapon of Mass Destruction)

My local newspaper recently ran this item:

"Methane gas from 90 flatulent cows exploded in a German farm shed, damaging the roof and injuring one of the animals, police reported. High levels of the gas had built up in the structure. ... then 'a static electric charge' caused the gas to explode into flames. One cow was treated for burns...."

I haven't been in a barn since Moses wore knee pants, but if memory serves, they were quite drafty. They also happened to have opened doors most of the time, thus eliminating the methane problem encountered in the German farm shed. Therefore, I've been pondering what might have been behind this explosion and how to prevent one from occurring in the future.

The first and most obvious solution is to feed each of the cows a quart of those little purple pills along with their grain. Or, the farmers could dissolve a gallon of Maalox in each water bucket. A solution for the German farmer is to replace the destroyed barn with one that is drafty. New isn't always better. Sometimes the old ways work better.

To avoid the "static electric charge," the farmer should equip each milking machine with a ground-fault interrupter. That way, instead of worrying about explosions, the farmer can go from milking station to milking station and push those little red buttons, worry free.

Very curious to me is how the methane built up enough gas to cause an explosion. Being a suspicious person, I think much more than cow farts caused the issue. My theory is that the cows wanted clover in their hay and shiny brass bells around their necks. They also splurged on weekly pedicures. Some even had artistic designs in their hoof polish. No more hosing down with cold water. These cows wanted rainfall showers and hot tubs with a massage to follow.

In order to afford these luxuries, the cows were operating a profitable, though dangerous, business in the barn. Tucked away in the space that formerly held a tractor was an opulent office with phones, computers and a nice shade tree. The manager in the hidden office was none other than Big Daddy Bull. He sold the cows' product to respectable looking middle men, who pretended to visit the farm to buy fresh milk.

In reality, the city folks lining up to Big Daddy's office were eager spenders of their hard-earned dollars on what the cows were really producing – high grade crystal meth milk. An accident in the production process resulted in a huge explosion. The farmer and the police were not eager to admit that the cows were smarter than they, and they did not want to admit that illegal activities were happening on their watch, so they said the explosion was sparked by pressurized cow farts.

Yeah, right! Like I am going to believe that.

All Grown Up and...

When I was a child, I was told that becoming an adult not only brought added responsibilities but also certain privileges such as drinking coffee and alcohol. I concede that the responsibilities part is true, but I'm here to tell you that the privilege part is not reality, at least not in my world.

Let's start with caffeine. Brewing coffee always smelled enticing to me, but the taste was nasty. You'd have thought someone had just given me something disgusting, like liquid liver.

When I visited friends and relatives who offered coffee, I politely declined, but nothing else was offered. When I was a young bride, I complained to my husband about this once, saying that I would have appreciated being offered an alternative. He asked, "Why didn't you ask for something else?

"Isn't that rude? If they had something else, they would have offered it."

"Many coffee drinkers just don't think of other options."

But he noted what I said. On future visits to friends and family, my husband would intercede for me. When I was offered coffee and declined, he would say, "She'd like a soda or water." The alternative was usually water.

As the years passed, I learned to drink tea saturated with lemon. But better, Pepsi was nectar from the gods. One day, the doctor told me that to control my blood pressure, I should stop drinking tea and soda. Despite thinking that two Pepsis and two cups of lemony tea a day were not much, I quit cold turkey. Have you ever seen a nice woman turn into the Wicked Witch of the West? That certainly did not work. After about three weeks, I was me again, unhappy, but no longer evil. You can guess why.

On two occasions, I attempted to make coffee, once for each of my husbands. Both endeavors were met with, "Don't ever touch my coffee pot again!"

Over the years, I kept a 4-cup pot and put a small coffee container in the freezer for my mother's visits. A few years ago on a trip to Minnesota, a friend and I stopped for gas. She said, "Let's get a latte. It doesn't taste like coffee." I agreed, and liked it! We bought another on the return trip.

Sometime after that trip, Ohio friends were coming to visit for a few days. Trying to be a good hostess, I asked another friend to buy some fresh coffee for them. On the way to the airport to pick up my visitors, I remembered that they used creamer. I stopped at the store to buy some. The dairy display case was overwhelming. I called my daughter for advice. She suggested some options. Selecting one, I approached the checkout but then remembered something else. Frantically calling her back, I said, "I'm on my way to the airport. Won't the creamer spoil?" She then directed me to the coffee aisle for a non-dairy selection.

After the arrival of my guests, one of my visitors made coffee and asked if I wanted some. Recalling the two lattes I'd enjoyed in Minnesota, I said, "Yes, if you can flavor it." She did. I added more flavor and enjoyed it. The next day she asked, "Would you like some more coffee in your cream?" I did. She then showed me how to brew my own coffee.

That was how I began to enjoy flavored coffee. That lasted for a couple years until a few months ago, when I had a major attack of vertigo. My doctor advised that part of my trouble was dehydration and that I should stop drinking caffeine beverages. She explained that caffeine is a diuretic and had contributed to my dehydration.

Is that why coffee drinkers drink so much coffee, I wondered. *They are in an endless downward spiral on a quest to quench thirst?*

For me, alcoholic beverages were a different story. The taste was pleasant as long the alcohol was in a mixed drink. My problem was that I was a cheap - and short - date. One drink made me happy, a second sent me to sleepy-by-land. So much for a fun night on the town.

Beer had its own peculiar consequences. One beer sends me running to the little girls' room to pray to the porcelain god. A co-worker once advised me, "Sharon, you are supposed to get drunk first, then throw up."

So, here I am again, a little girl who can't drink coffee or alcohol. I know it's better for my health, but gosh! I just want to have fun.

After a few years of reading about the benefits of coffee, I decided to give coffee drinking another try. So, I make a weakly flavored coffee and drink only one cup each day. My favorite coffee beverage, an occasional indulgence, is Starbuck's Java Chip – a summer treat, but only if I skip my morning cup of energy boost.

I'll look for a new approach to alcohol!

An Exercise Program that Works

Finally! I've figured out an exercise program that works. All I need to do is decide how to schedule around it. What is this wonderful program?

It's called the "Preschool Workout Regimen." When my great-grandsons are here (one at a time, thank goodness!), we sit and crawl around on the floor to play with cars, trucks and airplanes on my oval throw-rug. It has rings that allow for great races, tow-away zones and repair areas.

Then we play ball. The little ones' routines involve rolling or tossing soft balls in the house. This includes plenty of chasing the balls to wherever they land. The 4-year old prefers to take his hollow plastic ball and bat outside where we play baseball-golf-tennis. Since neither of us can pitch, this involves plenty of running or, in my case, walking to wherever the ball lands.

We're not good at hitting, either. Even though we take a batter's stance, we usually end up hitting the ball with a tennis backhand or teeing-off from the landing zone.

You'd think that Gramma, as a senior player, could hit and throw. No such luck! As an only child, I had no siblings available to teach me how to play ball. Physical education teachers skimmed over such lessons under the assumption that we all had those basic skills. Hah! Were they fooled!

The last time I was asked to play on a softball team, my reply was, "I can't run, and I throw like a girl." My frame of reference were the 1950s-60s girls, not the skilled athletes of today.

After a good lunch (Gramma remembers to eat healthy food in front of the little ones and is not saying what she eats other times), we go for a walk. This means that I pull a little boy and his supplies in a Radio Flyer with two seats, cup holders and a nylon roof on a three-mile trip to the outlet mall, around the complex and back home.

Sometimes we visit the farmers market or one of the local historic sites. That satisfies the wagon portion of the day and the need to fulfill the car and ball requirements.

After these activities, we usually have some quiet time, but not always. We may return to the racetrack on the oval rug until Mom or Mam-maw comes to take the little one home.

All I need to do now is decide how to turn this six-times a month routine into three times a week. Of course, that would mean leaving my job and eating less. Oh well, we can't win them all.

Blueberry Art – Bah! Humbug!

Last evening, our person decided to make one of her favorite dishes – walnut-cinnamon pancakes with blueberry topping. To that end, she opened the freezer and grabbed a bag of blueberries. Before our eyes, blueberries splattered across the freezer shelf, down the front of the refrigerator and across the floor. The bag clip had come off, leaving the bag wide open.

"Oh, drat!" she yelled and began picking up the berries and putting them back in the bag, the most convenient container, all the while wondering if the five-second rule applied. She kept thinking how much those blueberries cost and tried to tiptoe between the berries to protect us.

Half-frozen blueberries are hard to catch, slipping and sliding all over the place. It wasn't long before much more than five seconds had passed, and she had only picked up a few berries. Frustrated that she could no longer protect us, she waded into the scattered berries. Finally, all the berries were back in the bag and in the trash. The remaining juicy mess looked like a purple Jackson Pollock painting on her new floor. Well, it's three years old, but it was still new to her.

Next, still ignoring us, she grabbed a sponge and (famous-name-brand) cleaner and began wiping down the freezer and refrigerator. Incredibly, this worked, and soon the fridge was looking better than before. Even the fingerprints were gone. Then she retrieved her (famous-name-brand) mop, and she began to wash the floor from the outside in, keeping her fingers crossed that the purple art was erasable. She visualized a permanent stain that would leave her looking at the artwork for the next 20 years. All the while, she totally ignored us and our feelings.

Eventually, the mess was cleaned up. She then started to assess her appearance. Meanwhile, we, her white socks, were covered with tiny purple dots, looking like we'd strolled through Prince's "Purple Rain." Our bottoms looked like a tiny kitten had walked through a Jackson Pollock painting and then tap-danced on us. "No problem," she said. "These can be my "hang around the house" socks." Hang around the house socks. Indeed! How insulting!

To her, the worst of the disaster was her hands. From wrists to fingertips, they were purple, blue and black. OMG! She wouldn't be able to go out into public for at least a month. She had to try something.

First, she soaked the stained sponge in water and a thick layer of (famous-name-brand) dish cleaner, and then she began washing her hands with a huge glob of the same cleaner and warm water. She scrubbed and scrubbed until, finally, the colorful purple, blue and black had faded to a yucky gray with dark edges around her nails. Even the sponge, after rinsing, looked dark and tired, but usable.

Still thinking only of herself, she poured a bowl of white vinegar and soaked her hands for several more minutes. Finally, satisfied that she could enter polite society, she rinsed and dried her hands. Looking more carefully, she decided that a coat of nail polish would cover the remaining gray lines under her nails and detract from the gray tinges rimming her nail beds.

Satisfied with the result and smiling, she began to prepare for bed and tossed us in the laundry basket, no pretreatment, no bleach, no anything. And, here we still lie, 24 hours later!

At least we can take one bit of satisfaction: After all that muss and fuss, her walnut-cinnamon pancakes and blueberry topping were no longer on her mind. Her supper was two hard-boiled eggs and (not-a-famous-name-brand) tortilla chips. I know, but she said they were on sale.

Oops, I Hit the Wrong Key

I love writing but, regrettably, I have the typing skills of a St. Bernard, big paws and too much drool. This conflict has led me to some unusual experiences.

Back when we still used manual typewriters, my time was mostly spent tossing out wrecked pages and no longer usable carbon paper. Then we advanced to correcting typewriters. That was a big improvement. I could ruin carbon paper even faster. But the biggest advance for me was, as my friend once said, "You can type faster backward than forward." Not everyone can brag about that skill.

Eventually, we had computers in the workplace and were expected to work even faster. The good part was that I could edit on the screen and print out a clean copy for the boss. He was happy with that improvement. He just couldn't figure out why it took me five times longer to generate a letter than the other program assistants. Well, I was still typing backwards, so to speak. My right little finger is just a bit longer and wider than the left because it grew and developed strong muscles from repeated trips to the backspace key.

The biggest improvement was the internet. I could look up information for the boss and play Solitaire during my lunch break. Let's talk about the Solitaire first. It provided me with the opportunity to buy a whole new wardrobe. Since I no longer walked with my friends during our break, I became horizontally enhanced.

As for looking up information, while checking flights to Washington, D.C, I hit the wrong key and was taken to a site that burned my eyeballs and sent my brain into a catatonic state. Since I was incapable of retreating, I was at the site longer than was excusable as a typing mistake. I was told to pack my bags and leave immediately. How was I to know that watching porn on office time is considered a Class A work violation, no second chances?

That led to my early retirement. Because of my embarrassing dismissal, I was considered an undesirable potential employee. So now I write blogs and email my friends way too often. Those are mostly harmless hobbies, except when I hit the wrong key. I sent my pastor a video of a Mormon Tabernacle Choir performance, but he received a video of the same thing that got me fired from my job. Now I'm looking for a new church. How was I to know that hitting the wrong key is a mortal sin?

Christmas Newsletter

We all receive disgustingly cheerful newsletters listing dubious progeny accomplishments this time of year. Here is my contribution to the trend:

The holidays are upon us once again, and our family has much for which to be grateful. We are finishing our Christmas shopping and eager to place our gifts under the tree that Husband dragged home yesterday. I'm not sure where he found it, but it smells like he found it at the county landfill. This tree is so scraggly that even Charlie Brown would reject it. The good thing is that the tree was easy to decorate. A single string of lights runs straight up the trunk and ends just below the star that leans precipitously to starboard. We were able to toss two strands of tinsel onto the limb stub and get them to stick. We tried three, but three strands overloaded the stub and made the tree list to port.

Because of the economy, our gifts this year will be simple. Son #1 asked for a package of socks with extra wide tops to warm the lovely ankle bracelet generously given him by the judge. He finds the ankle bracelet attractive, but he fusses about the frostbite that afflicts his leg when he goes outside to smoke. Additionally, he has started a trend by inspiring his friends and siblings to achieve his greatness. Already, three of his "buds" are sporting their own ankle bracelets. They gleefully text each other about the phone calls they receive from the police department when the bracelets set off bells at the station. It is a competition.

Son #2 is aspiring to earn his own bracelet, but, so far, he has only achieved receiving probation. He is requesting extra wide-top socks so that he will be prepared when his turn for an ankle bracelet is approved. He also has requested an ergonomic pillow for study hall naps. Classmates have learned not to criticize his snoring. His nap habit has contributed greatly to the economy as the school nurse's office must keep a large stock of nose bandages.

We are so proud that Daughter #1 is achieving greatness at her high school. She passed chorus this year when the choir director generously agreed to accept her reggae version of "Stairway to Heaven" as an entry in the school's alma mater contest. Luckily, the academic advisor has decided that she no longer needs to pass such courses as biology, math or history, so she will be graduating two years early. This daughter was easy to shop for, because she just asked for a year's supply of black nail polish, black lipstick and green hair dye.

Daughter #2 won honors for selling the most Girl Scout cookies in her troop. She accomplished this by blackmailing her middle school teachers. I'm not sure where she found all that salacious information, but our family had fun reading it. It's too bad the teachers bought the cookies, because we'd really love to share these stories with the school administrators. No shopping problem here either. This daughter requested a gift card to Slut-Mart.

Husband is doing very well. He was presented Slacker of the Year award by his company. They said he is slacking so well, that if he keeps up the good work, he'll be given a permanent vacation. Can you imagine how much fun we'll have with all that spare time?

As for me, I'm learning how to cook without setting off the smoke alarm. It only paged the fire department once this week when I baked brownies for Daughter #2's Girl Scout party. The girls smiled bravely as they gazed at the brownies and held tissues over their noses to protect the tray of well-done brownies from their cold germs. They are so generous! They showed this by tossing the entire tray into the snow to feed the birds. I am so proud.

Happy Holidays to you and your family! We hope your year has been as wonderful as ours!

Director of Capture Management

This job title is what I saw in a two column, eleven-inch advertisement in my newspaper's classified section. *

My first thoughts were: "Huh?" and "What's that?" Before I could read the job description, my mind ranged over several possibilities such as:

- Seal Team Six needs a new leader.
- FBI wants to actually catch those folks whose photos appear at the post office.
- Transportation Safety is hoping to catch all those nail clippers that slide through airport metal detectors.
- Nigerian bankers are angry that we aren't responding to their pleas for money.
- School truancy officers need a manager.
- Counties want to catch more unleashed dogs.
- Lucky Charms is still searching for the Leprechaun.
- The British still have a bounty on Captain Jack Sparrow.

I could go on, but these examples should help you understand what circuits my brain impulses traveled to find an answer. I'm not the least bit embarrassed. I'm pleased that my brain still functions in "silly" mode.

So, what is the job? I'm not sure, but the ad contains words and phrases like "unmanned systems," "defense," "civil and commercial," and "active secret clearance or higher." All are, obviously, not describing a job for which I am qualified. Oh well, maybe next time, after I learn how to use a computer for something besides writing silly blogs.

*Grabble, an advertising supplement to the Daily Press, May 29, 2011

Dirt Fairy

Sometime in the past few days, the dirt fairy visited my house. A dirt fairy is a little like Tinkerbell, but instead of visiting Neverland, he or she visits good boys and girls when they are not at home and fills their planter boxes full of nice, rich soil.

What motivates a dirt fairy? This was a mystery to be solved. But where to start?

The planter box itself was a surprise. When son Dan visited in early December, I mentioned that I was considering taking up several bricks from my patio and using them to construct a planter box. The following day, Dan purchased the necessary supplies, including stones for drainage, and he constructed a lovely 5'x2'x3' planter box. My job was to stain the wood to match my deck.

Returning to the fairy mystery: I called Pilot, to whom I had subtly hinted that a load of dirt compost from the county composting site would be nice. Subtle, huh? I just came right out and asked, not once, but four or five times. Each time we discussed delivery logistics, and we came to the same non-conclusions.

How does your schedule look for next week? Can we do this without scratching the truck?

When I asked if he brought the soil, Pilot laughed and said that the dirt elves brought it. He continued, "Dan must have contacted the elves and told them to bring the dirt." That response made me certain that he had made the delivery intending it to be a birthday surprise. I called him sneaky. To which, Pilot insisted that, seriously, it was not he who had brought it.

My next guess was that my daughters had snuck the dirt into the box while I wasn't looking. I called Linda and left a bubbly, grateful message. She didn't return my call. Just as I was preparing to telephone her twin sister, Sarah, my phone rang.

"It was us, Mom," Linda said. "We were planning to surprise you for your birthday. You usually walk around oblivious to what is happening around you; so, we thought we could pull it off."

They know this from experience. One time they changed my kitchen faucets and I didn't notice until four days later – after they told me what they had done.

This time I have the satisfaction of knowing that I found a "secret" before they told me where to look. Mom still has it going on upstairs, at least sometimes.

Dragon Herding

I have the most challenging job in the world. I herd dragons. My job is to keep order among the dragons in our corrals. Believe me, that is one tough job.

Dragons are naturally rambunctious critters. They fly around when you want them to stay put, sort of like three-year-old children. They fight over who has the shiniest coat and who has the biggest fangs. When they start flame-throwing contests, you'd better hide or, at least, run for your flame-retardant suit. NASCAR doesn't own enough suits to keep me supplied. Have you ever tried to lift a fire extinguisher large enough to douse a dragon's belch? Not easy, I tell you!

One time, a striped, purple-and-green dragon almost ate my arm for lunch. I didn't jump away fast enough when I threw a goat into his corral. Luckily, I ran fast and the doctor only needed 40 sutures and a bandage to repair my arm. Another important safety measure is that a herder must *never* go to work with beer-breath. Alcohol and flames do not lead to a happy ending.

If you think that's bad, you should see the dragons when they begin imbibing! They don't care whose beer they steal, as long as there is plenty of it. If there aren't enough beer barrels to go around, the dragons begin rioting. They fuss and fight, swish their giant tails and throw flames all over the place. That's when you have to try to herd them back to their gigantic dragon corrals. Herding sober dragons is hard enough, but when they're drunk, they fall all over the place, singe each other's wings and roar loud enough to be heard across the ocean.

On top of that, they don't like to sort themselves out by type and color. That's something I must do, because dragon aficionados, just like horse owners, have their favorite breeds and colors. One problem is that big black dragons don't want to associate with small green ones or middle-sized blue ones, but they also don't want to be separated. They like to mingle so they can fight when they feel like it. I know a dragon who has been in so many fights that he no longer has any hide left. However, that hasn't stopped him. He's still in there biting, kicking, snarling and throwing flames.

Thankfully, I have assistants who help me. Fairies fly around the rowdy dragons and attempt magic spells to calm them. Sometimes it works, but, occasionally, even fairy magic isn't enough. Unicorns assist with round-ups to prepare the dragons for sale. The unicorns surround the dragons, separate them by breed and color and then escort them into their separate corrals. These magical creatures do their best, but even when the dragons are compliant, unicorn magic doesn't always work. It only takes one hyper-active dragon who skipped his tranquilizer hay to start a ruckus. Then away we go again.

This is a never-ending job. Talk about stressful! My doctor keeps telling me to get a quieter job. I suppose she's right. However, dragon herders are paid extremely well and get excellent benefits. For example, no other company can touch our medical and life insurance plans. Even with all these hazards, I would never give up my job. I just can't see myself doing boring jobs like bull-riding or sky-diving.

Driver's License Woes

My day was going pretty well until I opened my mail.
That cannot be me!

They must have put a much older woman's photo on my new driver's license. This woman looks old, with wrinkles and age spots. Even worse, the photo is black and white; i.e., shades of gray on a beige background. Those are old people colors. They don't accent my sparkly, hazel eyes or my hair, whatever color it is. To add more insults, the license is marked that I must wear corrective lenses and use a side mirror because I'm hearing impaired. Sounds like a conspiracy to make us young chicks think we are old.

But maybe they're right. After all, I am officially old. The DMV had required me to visit their testing site and peer into that little binocular thing and read line number 2. The woman passed me without a smile, typed all the valid information into the computer and accepted my check. Perhaps her furry hat was pinching her smile button.

I smiled at her and commented that she was really busy that day. She just responded that it was a normal day – without smiling. I'm sure it was. Our local DMV office has only half of its eight customer stations staffed. When I arrived, people had already filled most of the chairs, and a long line wound its way to the check-in station. The same was true while I waited and when I left.

After moaning and groaning, I slid the temporary license into my wallet and lifted my spirits by recalling this morning's play date with Jonathan. We had a lot of fun, but his mother may shoot me tomorrow.

Since the temperatures were cold, we stayed inside. We played softball with an inflatable ball. Then we built a fort using a recliner and an upholstered chair topped with a flannel sheet. Sofa pillows and fleece throws added to the fort's comfort. Jonathan preferred to call it a house.

Playing inside the fort was restrictive and boring, so Jonathan found a more interesting thing to do. He asked me to crawl under the structure and sit in the soft chair. He carefully centered a blue linen napkin on the roof. Then he jumped on it and crashed the fort down.

I helped by tossing whatever blankets remained on top of him. He crawled out of the mess and then begged me to build a new house, over and over again.

Mom will likely be angry when Jonathan starts to pull the blankets off his bed to make a "house." Hey, what are great-grammas for, if not for fun?

Besides, if I am a kid like this, I don't need to worry about that old lady photograph on my driver's license!

I Did It Wrong

After my babies started coming two at a time, I decided it was time to do some serious family planning. I was fertile during the dark ages when birth control pills and IUDs were still the latest and greatest technology. Depro-Provera was not even a gleam in a woman's eye.

After taking the pills for the maximum number of years considered safe, I switched to other methods of birth control on the advice of my doctor. These methods all did the job, but not all were, shall we say, fun and easy to use. I even tried the orange juice method. *What is that*, you ask? I asked the doctor the same question. "Do I drink the OJ before or after?" He looked at me like I was an idiot and said, "Instead."

Now, after all these years of purchasing expensive contraception items, I learned that there are better and less expensive family planning methods. I cheered, knowing my daughters and granddaughters won't have to go through the trial-and-error methods that I had used.

Amazing discoveries happen daily. For instance, a few months ago, a politician said that women cannot conceive from rape because stress will prevent conception! But the most amazing information comes from Saudi Arabia where a conservative cleric made this proclamation about mechanical birth control: He said, "If a woman drives a car, not out of pure necessity, that could have negative physiological impacts, as functional and physiological medical studies have shown that this automatically affects the ovaries and pushes the pelvis upwards." *

Just imagine, I could have avoided all that hassle and money by simply going for a daily drive! Back then, gas prices varied from $.29 to $1.00 per gallon, much less expensive than contraceptive products. It would also have given me short serenity breaks as I cruised along country roads admiring the corn, wheat and soy beans. With the windows down, I could have heard the birds singing and felt the wind blowing through my long red tresses. My husband would have been delighted to come home to a calm, collected wife, instead of one who was exhausted from chasing children all day.

What a wondrous discovery this cleric has made, and he's not even a doctor or scientist. Some day we might celebrate Driving Prevents Babies Day. Future generations of women will no longer need to spend hours in the gynecologist's waiting room, wondering what antiquated contraception they will be told to use this time. Instead, they can look forward to pleasant drives around the countryside, smelling the flowers, admiring the butterflies and going home to a houseful of children.

*News of the Weird, The Daily Press, October 17, 2013, Reuters news release

How to Feel like a Fool and Get your Dishwasher Fixed

Ever since I bought my dishwasher many years ago, it has made a thunking noise and has required an extra push to get the door to seal. Assuming it was made that way, I continued to push, and it continued to thunk. Events aligned to get it fixed last week, and I only had to make a fool of myself to get it done.

My writing group was scheduled to meet at my house, and I needed to do a little bit of touch-up cleaning. I pulled out my handy-dandy, Swiffer duster and began to dust. I poked that long-handled gift from the cleaning fairies under, between and over dusty surfaces. I was so inspired that I dusted things that had not been touched since the first Bush administration. The remaining dust appeared to pre-date the Stone Age, so I decided to let it continue its progress toward making a new planet.

I worked my way through the whole house and finished with the refrigerator top. I took a step back to better reach what was left. Wham! I was sitting on the dishwasher door, bottom rack and dishes waiting to be put away. Colorful metaphors issued rapid-fire from my mouth. I just knew the appliance would need to be replaced.

Shifting my weight to stand and inspect the damage, I noticed that a dinner fork was dangling from my left thumb. I pulled out the three embedded tines and headed for the bathroom to slap on a Band Aid, leaving bright red splotches along the way. It looked like I had left a trail of melted, cherry popsicle drippings instead of bread crumbs to find my way back home.

Washing off the mess, I applied standard first aid, and, after taking a queasy-break, I texted my daughter to ask her to stop over when she had a chance to make sure I had bandaged my wound properly. She agreed to come a few hours later since she was currently babysitting her grandchildren.

I needed a shower badly, so after the dizziness and bloodshed had abated, I decided to give it a try. I could wash my body one-handed, but not my messy hair. Trying to find a solution, I worked and worked to get a finger protector on my thumb. By the time I finally rolled it down to the thumb's base, I was again leaking vital fluids. I cut off the original bandage and the protector.

After taking another queasy-break, I again bandaged the leaky thumb. This time I added a vinyl glove and headed to the shower. Somehow, I cleaned my body; however, let me ask you this: Have you ever tried to shampoo and condition your hair with one hand? I lathered here, then there, and then another place, hoping all the hair was clean. I rinsed and repeated the procedure with the wash-out conditioner. Toweling myself dry with one hand was another interesting experience. Finally, I attempted to apply leave-in conditioner. How much hair was actually covered is a good question.

A few hours later, my daughter arrived and inspected the still leaking thumb. She drove to the closest drugstore and bought me some waterproof band aids. She redressed the wound and prepared to leave. I asked her to check my dishwasher for damage because it was making new thunks and clunks. Inspecting the machine, she found that a screw was missing. She replaced it, and now the dishwasher closes properly with just a click.

Overall, I think my wound method turned out to be cheaper than a dishwasher repair bill. At least, that is my consolation.

I'm an Artist

I received one of those eagerly anticipated letters from my Home Owners Association that began by saying that my house was lovely. (I suppose they ignored my weedy flower garden and my splintery deck.) However, they suggested a few tweaks to come into neighborhood compliance. Most of the suggestions required stain or paint.

Dutifully, I went to the store to buy deck stain, door paint and brushes. I have plenty of can openers and stir sticks. In fact, I have enough to keep my paint cans open and stirred until I reach the point of hiring the job out to a lesser artist than me. My largest purchase was a gross of edging tape to help me stay within the lines. I carefully taped anything that was even close to another color. Then I donned my safety glasses and plastic gloves to spruce up my house.

The deck and front porch are now a new color, yet close to the old shade. I am required to stay within the HOA color guidelines. I changed the front door from the dark red that it has proudly worn for the past 12 years to a lovely forest green that matches the house number plaque I purchased at Busch Garden's Christmas Market a year and half ago.

After a few weeks of work, an hour here and there, the project was complete. I carefully removed the edging tape. This was a sad duty, because I was beginning to like that blue outline. I thought it set off the other colors and made my house more cheerful than my neighbors' houses. Once that task was completed, I stood back to admire my work. I noticed that, while my edges were all neat, several drips, splashes and smudges had made the siding and door frames look like a Jackson Pollock painting. What an exciting prospect! If Pollock could sell his drips and splashes for thousands of dollars, why shouldn't I get at least a million for a work of art that included a two-bedroom house?

Regrettably, all I got was another letter from the HOA telling me to get some paint that matches the siding to cover up the various drips, splashes and smudges. Some people just don't appreciate valuable art!

Life in the Cold Lane

So many have come down with mystery viruses this winter; but not me. I was special. I developed a virus from H-E-double hockey sticks. No traditional symptoms for me, nope. I just sneezed and coughed hard enough to scare anyone within hearing range. While cruising down aisle five at My Food is Cheaper than Yours, my cough erupted. When I was finally able to inhale, I heard somebody in the meat department yelling, "Incoming!"

I tried to take precautions to avoid spreading the joy. You should have seen me pushing my cart through the pharmacy section. I had the smaller, double-decker cart. The top basket contained six 1,000-count boxes of Kleenex, all open, and a 13-gallon trash bag to catch the used tissues. The bottom basket held a gallon bottle of hand sanitizer with a hose that coiled around the basket supports and ended at the baby seat. The sprayer was set on "Deluge."

Due to my almost continuous use of said products, my nose and mouth were firmly planted in the upper-arm portion of my jacket to avoid accidents. The sight of this caused small children to ask anxiously, "Mommy, why is that lady hiding her face? Is this a robbery?" The mothers who looked like they'd seen the Big Guy from the hot place replied, "No, Sweetie, that's the cold monster, and she's here to give us all something horrid."

After loading my basket with more Kleenex, trash bags, hand sanitizer and a half-bushel of Ricola, I headed toward the last checkout lane. You know that lane. No one goes there because the walk is too far. The clerk scanned everything with her little remote gadget and accepted my money with tongs and called for a supervisor to exchange her till. She didn't call for a bagger; instead, she pointed to the plastic bags and said, "Use those bags, but please don't recycle them."

As for me, I went home and began toking my nebulizer like it was a giant roll-your-own. This past week has gone fast just inhaling and eating pizza and brownies. I'm well enough to try an outing tomorrow in the trees and grass, but I'm really going to miss the nebulizer buzz.

Meeting Deadlines

I just received an email from my editor requesting a short article about alternative healing. "Sure, I'll be glad to do that," I replied. "Tuesday will be fine," he said.

Today is Wednesday so I have plenty of time. Rather than procrastinating, I get started immediately.

My first task is to identify expert sources. I start a list: Barb for massage; Bettina for regeneration; George for reconnection; Carolyn for neuro-structural therapy and holographic reprogramming; and Quinn for yoga therapy. They're all good sources. Can I include them all in this short article? Or should I ask Gary, the editor, if I can do several short pieces featuring one healing modality at a time? M-m-m-m.

Let me eat some lunch and think about it. I have plenty of time. I go to the kitchen and fix a large salad and sit down with my plate and the newspaper. Lunch is finished, but I want to finish reading this section before I start writing.

Now the after-lunch sedation is kicking in. It's time for a quick nap.

I wake feeling refreshed, but somehow it is 4:30, and everyone's workday is done. I'll call my sources in the morning. In the meantime, I sit down and email Gary for clearer instructions. I have accomplished an important step. Enough work for today! Let's watch what is left of the Oprah show and catch the early news.

Thursday – The day dawns bright and cheery. I have to hurry to get to the walking-group site on time. My daughter and I walk the 2.2 miles and chat about the story I will write and how to develop it. I'm getting excited now. I have a concept. But wait! I must make quick stops at the library, the bank and the post office. My errands are done. Now it is time for a fast lunch before my support group meeting. Finally, it is late afternoon, I'm home, and the newspaper is calling.

Friday – I must make those calls, but that darn phone weighs at least 500 pounds. I should have a hearty breakfast first. With a full tummy, I sit down with my list and look up the phone numbers. Oh, I'd better check my email to see what Gary said about one long article or several short ones. He said he wants one article, but it can go a little longer than usual.

Back to the phone list. Who to call first? Oh well, let me just start at the top. I call all five sources, but only two are available to talk. I do short interviews with them and leave messages for the rest. Well, I can't start writing until I have all the interviews, so this is a good time to wash the dishes and clean the bathroom.

Saturday – Walking group again. Returning to the recreation center, I learn that Barb is leading a drumming therapy session, so I'll stop and join in. That will surely energize me to write. Barb asks how the article is coming. I tell her that everyone has returned my calls and I plan to start writing this afternoon, leaving plenty of time to edit before Tuesday. She agrees that is a good plan. Barb leads this disparate group of drummers, some talented and some rhythmically challenged, in an energizing session. We all leave with our hearts pounding and our faces shining with joy. This is too much energy to waste at the computer! Let me go upstairs and work out for a while. Now I'm tired. Lunch and a nap sound good.

Sunday - The paper is full of great articles and, of course, the comics. I must read them, but first I need to shower and get ready for the 10 a.m. meeting. When the meeting ends, I'm hungry. I fix a salad and sit down to read the paper. The next thing I know, I've worked my way through all the sections that interest me and have come to the comics. But, I'm sleepy, so I'll take a nap. When I awaken, it's time to call my mom. She expects me to call each Sunday. We have a nice phone visit, but she reports that she is having trouble with her eyes. Now, I'm too upset to write. Let me watch something totally inane like "The Simpsons" to lift my spirits.

Monday – I really must get at the story. Today is cold. Let me fix a cup of tea to warm my body and my mind. Carolyn calls. She asks if it is too late to change her comments. "Not at all," I say as I pull out my notes to update her information. Now, I've done something productive today and can relax. I decide to wash the kitchen floor and then review my notes.

Oh! It's almost time for my book study group. I shower, fix supper and review our reading assignment so I can sound like I know what I'm talking about when we discuss the chapter.

Tuesday morning – It is beautiful outside, but I can't enjoy it. I have to get this article written. I fix myself a quick bowl of cereal and sit down at the computer. I re-read the notes and finally make a decision about how to approach the topic and who to list first, second, and third, etc. I begin typing and draft a pretty good article. It's lunch time and my stomach is growling, so I fix a sandwich and decide I need a quick nap before I edit the article.

Four o'clock – An hour is plenty of time to edit. I sit down and read what I have written, change some wording here, rearrange persons two and three, run spell-check, and read again. Did I catch the personalities involved and the uniqueness of each healing modality? This seems to cover the topic well.

I go to email, attach the article and send it off to Gary. I did a good job. It is now 4:55. I beat the 5 p.m. deadline with five minutes to spare.

Thank God I didn't procrastinate!

Surprising News

This morning I opened my email and began reading messages. Suddenly I saw this big headline:

"You should always consult with a physician before beginning any treatment for erectile dysfunction."

Below was a photo of a handsome young man and a beautiful young woman obviously anticipating their impending pleasure. In the upper left corner, the ad showed a blossom of three pills (Cialis, Levitra and Viagra) all pointing out with a red dot in the center and a caption reading:

"From $0.62 - Special Price – Order Now: Men's Trial Pack"

Then the picture shifted to a huge jet with its nose pointed at me, implying that I would soon have great elevation. This message was shorter:

"Fast World-Wide Delivery!"

This ad might have been good news to some, but, it deflated my self-image. You see, I don't have any body parts that need enhancement. I gave birth to three children, performed what has traditionally been considered women's work and acted in ways that defined me as a woman.

But wait! This morning that email told me I am a man. Can this be true? Many people have told me that on-line advertisers target their ads to a specific audience who will use their products, so it must be true.

Do I need to buy tighty-whities instead of lacy undergarments and start watching sports and playing fantasy football? Perhaps I should take a lesson from my grandfather's philosophy: "I don't curse, drink or chew, nor associate with women who do." I might do well with the skill he taught me - how to roll cigarettes.

What's a gal, er, guy, to do?

No More Ads, Please!

Several weeks ago, I received an ad for male enhancement medication. I thought the concept was funny, so I wrote a blog about it. I thought that I had made it clear that I'm a female and have no use for those products.

However, the internet seems to believe otherwise. Every day I receive several advertisements for those products. Even worse, I receive messages from both males and females looking for a good time. I delete the messages immediately without opening them.

Yet, they keep coming and coming. Oops, this message is starting to sound like what I'm trying to avoid.

What is the solution? Mmm, perhaps I should buy a sample packet of the male enhancement meds, toss them in the trash, and then write a customer dis-satisfaction review. I can explain in detail how the product didn't work and post it all over Facebook and other social media sites. Oooh, sweet revenge!

With my luck, that would only draw more attention. Each manufacturer might send me free samples with instructions about how to enhance their effectiveness. I might get more emails from good time seekers offering their assistance for a fee.

I can't use the products. I don't want a good time for a fee. What's a girl to do?

Officially Old

Life moves along at warp speed. We're in first grade, then married with children, children leave home, college begins, career follows, and, maybe, a second or third to go in new directions. Then comes semi-retirement and enjoying time with grand- and great-grandchildren. Hopefully, semi-retirement will become full retirement with hours of fun with the great-grands and perhaps some traveling to see the United States' natural wonders.

I look at varicose veins as leg art, no tattoos required. I see wrinkles as character lines created by life. Most of them are laugh lines. Even though my red hair is fading into the "other blonde," I consider it a mark of maturity. Each of those OB (other blonde) hairs was earned through life experiences. They are a sign that I lived life as fully as I was able. And, perhaps, the water on my brain has drained away. *

I walk a bit slower, but that gives me time to enjoy the beautiful flowers of summer. Getting up and down from the floor is now a major effort, a good reminder of my age each time I play on the floor with my great-grands. The flab under my arms is just the beginning of wings. Soon they will grow, and I will be able to fly wherever I wish to go.

At least, that was the way I viewed my life until I was approached by a small child two days ago.

All of this is just a lead-in to the words that could have seared my soul, but instead gave me a good laugh at the different ways small children and older adults perceive life.

I was working in the Magic Shop at Busch Gardens Williamsburg, greeting customers, chatting about this and that and ringing up their purchases. All was well in my world. Then a little girl about six or seven years old approached me and asked, "Are you old?"

"Yes. Why do you ask?"

"Because you look old."

Now it's official. I've been declared old, not just fluffy and mature.

*When I was in elementary and middle school, the other students used to say, "Sharon's hair is red because she has water on the brain and her hair fell in and rusted."

Pants on Fire!

You know the first part of that saying. That's what I was thinking as I was trying to follow Google Maps to a city I'd never visited to pick up my copy of *Go Set a Watchman* by Harper Lee. I ordered the book months ago when Books-A-Million offered a pre-sale option and I didn't know the Williamsburg store was going to close. I checked back shortly before the closing date and the local staff assured me that I'd be mailed a copy of the book on the release date.

It's several days past the release date, and no book has arrived. I looked on the B-A-M website to find the nearest store, which is in Colonial Heights, one hour and nine minutes west of here. There are others about the same drive time away, but I thought this option would give me an opportunity to take a leisurely drive on scenic roads to a new city. I'd previously driven about 45 minutes of the predicted 69-minute journey, so felt confident I could find my way the other 24 minutes without a problem.

You need to know that since Virginia was the first English colony, locations have unusual names and roads were constructed on colonial wagon trails (meaning curvy) and that counties didn't come into existence until much later. Thus, I left my home in James City County and wound my way into the countryside, crossing the Chickahominy River and enjoying the beautiful scenery and the sunshine. (Only Colonial Williamsburg is built on a grid. Governor Frances Nicholson may have been lacking in statesman skills, but he knew how to build a city a mile long and four streets wide.)

I passed through Charles City County, seeing several colonial plantations along the way. By the time I came to a road change, a light rain began falling. I crossed the James River at the Benjamin Harrison Bridge and headed to Hopewell. By then the rain was coming down in sheets, and I was hoping that I could read the signs well enough to make my turns. I made two turns correctly.

The map indicated that after 3.5 miles, I was to turn left on Winston Churchill Drive, which did not reveal itself by the time I'd gone almost 4 miles. I pulled into a Subway and asked the clerk how to find that street. She said that it was at the intersection just a few yards away. I turned where she indicated, but the sign said 6th Street.

I decided to trust her and continued driving until the end of the street. At that point, a right turn put me onto Winston Churchill Drive. By this time the rain had let up and I was able to follow directions again, travelling on Oaklawn and Woodlawn Drives without making a turn or even changing lanes.

Finally, I reached the mall where the book store was located but couldn't find the store. After walking into the mall and asking three men for directions, a janitor told me how to find Books-A-Million – around a curve and across the street. I followed his directions, and in no time I was at the book store. Five minutes later I was back in my car.

I left the mall and began driving back down the road. I found an exit to I-95 South that would take me to Raleigh, NC. I knew that was the right general direction and that eventually I'd find an exit that would bring me back to Williamsburg. The rain had once again turned into a downpour, but the interstate signs were large enough to read in the rain.

Ah, a treasure loomed – a route to the Benjamin Harrison Bridge - and even the rain eased. After another few miles, I saw familiar territory and began to breathe normally. Soon the rain stopped. I enjoyed music while scanning the lovely plantation route, eventually reaching Williamsburg. As I neared, the sound system came alive with the Beatles' song "Help!" I laughed and said, "You're a little late. I'm only a block from home now."

I made that 2-hour-18 minute-round trip (plus 5 minutes in the store) in 3 hours and 11 minutes. What do you think? Did I make good time or receive bad driving directions?

Tooth Fairy - Changed Tactics

It used to be that the Tooth Fairy gave boys and girls money for their teeth. Now she charges for her services. How did that come to be? I'm not sure, but this is my story and I'm sticking to it.

My parents grew up during the Great Depression. When they lost their baby teeth, they were handed a clean rag to bite down on and received compliments about growing up. By the 1950s, when I lost my primary teeth, Tooth Fairy left me a dime for my first tooth and a nickel for the second. After that, I was given a Kleenex and congratulated on my achievement. When I asked for money for the other teeth that had fallen out, TF scolded me for attempted extortion. Actually, the lack of cash was beneficial: no money, no candy, no cavities.

> Dear Big Tooth Fairy
> I lost a tooth that I didn't even no it was loose.
>   Love,
>   Little Tooth
> P.S. Please give me 25¢ and write me a rhume.

Along came the 1970s, and my children were more sophisticated. They wrote notes to TF requesting a quarter and a rhyme.

Their efforts paid off. The Tooth Fairy left them 50 cents for their first tooth and 25 cents thereafter. Still not a fortune, but at least she shelled out for each tooth and took time to write a short funny verse.

The Tooth Fairy had to fly to Germany to look under my grandchildren's pillows. Since TF has small wings, I'm guessing that she had to buy airline tickets for those trips. She couldn't have had much cash left after all those trans-oceanic trips. Even so, I'm sure my grandchildren made out well.

Now my four oldest great-grandsons are keeping her busy, dropping dollar bills under pillows, even for a tooth that slid down one little boy's throat while he was eating. Other teeth have been dropped on the way to their pillows, but "The Molinator" * still deposits cash for every tooth.

I understand that inflation costs the Tooth Fairy more each generation. Everything else costs more. Why not teeth? However, I don't understand why Tooth Fairy is now charging me to retrieve my recently lost tooth. Did she go broke serving all those little children? Was it a dollar fine for each time I forgot to brush my teeth at bedtime?

All I can do is explain how it all happened. A few months ago, during my regular check-up, my dentist gasped when he saw my x-ray. A cavity had formed under a crown on a 12-year molar. After assuring me that I was not ready to face a toothless old-age, he explained that this was a job for Tooth Fairy and that she would need to return to dental college to learn how to replace a tooth.

After her graduation with an advanced degree, TF began a procedure that included multiple x-rays and all sorts of strange equipment. The most traumatic event was her extraction of my infected tooth. When TF realized that I snore like a saw mill and that my exhalations have the power of a hurricane, she decided not to try a sleep extraction but to use an ordinary numbing medication.

She stabbed me several times with a syringe filled with happy juice. After a few minutes, I was lying in the reclining chair and smiling up at her with a cotton filled mouth. She firmly grasped the tooth and began tugging. Nothing happened. She tried again, wiggling the tooth a bit, then she wiggled harder and still nothing. She grabbed a chisel and a hammer and broke the tooth in two. Soon TF was leaning over me, tugging with all her might. Finally, she climbed on my chest to get a better grip, bracing my jaw with her knee to keep it from dislocating. Finally, the first half of the tooth popped out, almost banging TF on her own chin from her exertion. The second half slid out easily.

After all that, TF inserted a temporary replacement tooth in the empty space. From the sounds and her motions, I could visualize what was happening. First, she used a Black and Decker electric drill to make a hole in the jaw bone. That didn't take long. Then TF inserted a place-holder peg with a ratchet wrench. As her hand moved back and forth to tighten the peg, I felt like my mouth was under construction. When she completed this phase of my oral repairs, I told TF what I had imagined. She confirmed my suspicion by saying that was exactly what had happened. Then she explained that she had honed her skills at home by making wee doll houses with a full range of tiny construction tools. That analogy remained in my mind this morning when TF inserted my new tooth, ratcheted the permanent peg into place and sealed it with a caulking gun. Oh, the surface material is partially zirconium, so I now have a fake diamond smile. I even have a specially designed tooth brush. It looks like a teeny, tiny bottle brush.

When I asked for a dollar for my lost tooth, Tooth Fairy just rolled on the floor laughing. She reminded me that children's teeth simply become loose and fall out. She just plucks the clean, dry tooth from under pillows. For all the trouble I gave her, she demanded the title to my car and a second mortgage on my home. I'm sure the new tooth will be worth all the cost and effort. But, gosh, I can't even go around to my friends and say, "See my new tooth." It's just not polite behavior for woman who has long since passed her ninth birthday.

*From the *"Santa Claus"* movie series

Who Hid the Chocolate?

Many of us have addiction issues. They can lead to tragedy, or they can lead to laughter. Here's my story:

Several years ago, I was fighting a sugar and chocolate addiction. Following the suggested protocol by multiple 12-step programs, I totally abstained from anything that remotely resembled a dessert. This was, indeed, a white-knuckle existence.

So, while clenching my teeth and trying to smile, I kindly asked my family to please keep their desserts out of the house. I didn't care if they ate Reese's Cups or Hershey bars until the cows came home, if they didn't do it in front of me – and brushed their teeth before I saw them.

Because of this addiction, deprivation and approaching menopause, my nose became an ultra-sensitive tracking device. That summer, my hubby's son came to live with us before entering college. Hubby explained the house rules to him: pick up after yourself, do your own laundry and, for God's sake, don't eat candy in the house.

Thinking this was a silly rule, the darling lad walked to the neighborhood gas station and came home with two candy bars. Hubby told him to get rid of them, or I'd go ballistic. The boy, being more rational than I, didn't want to gobble down two candy bars in addition to the one he'd eaten on the way home. He decided to hide the candy where I'd never find it.

Several hours later, I came home from work, and, debating about what to cook for supper, I opened the freezer to scan the contents. No sooner had the door cracked open, when I let out a yell, "WHO PUT THE CHOCOLATE IN THE FREEZER?"

No answer, but from the living room I heard gales of laughter, high fives and "I told you so, son! You owe me a Pepsi." I stomped into the living room demanding an explanation or all the hilarity.

Hubby said, "I told him your nose is as sensitive to chocolate as a hound's is to a rabbit, but he didn't believe me. He just knew he could hide the candy where you couldn't find it."

"But, why the freezer?"

"Because freezing dulls scents."

"That makes sense," I said, "if the item has been frozen for at least a century."

I explored further and found the offending candy bars on top of a chuck roast, under a pork roast and totally hidden by stacks of hamburger patties. Not enough meat to hide a chocolate scent from me, though. I removed the candy and handed it to the still grinning young man and told him to hide them in his sock drawer.

That would disguise any odor.

Twins – Oh, no!

Recently I was admiring some sweet boy twins. That triggered a flashback to when my twins were born. So, I'm taking this opportunity to inflict - excuse me - to share my memories with you.

The year was 1967, and Daddy was on his second tour in Vietnam. His first tour had been when our son was born. That man had great timing!

I was very pregnant and wondering if our baby would ever be born. There were no sonograms back then, just x-rays that doctors used judiciously on pregnant moms. They had chosen not to use them on me. I awoke before dawn needing to use the "necessary". When that task was completed, I felt a sharp contraction, and five minutes later, another. After 30 minutes, I called the doctor and my parents, waking them all from a sound sleep. My mother drove me to the hospital, luckily only a few blocks away. My father drove my three-days-short-of-18-months-old son to his aunt's house for day care before he went to work.

By this time, the contractions were coming quickly and forcefully. I checked in and was given papers to sign. "You expect me to sign my name?" I complained. "I can barely breathe, much less hold a pen!"

The staff put me in a labor room with another woman who was sitting calmly and reading a magazine. Not knowing if she was a "first-timer" and not wanting to frighten her, I kept my lips tightly sealed. No moans or groans, much less screams, came from my half of the room.

After a few minutes, the nurse wheeled me into the delivery room without the normal pre-delivery preparations. She said there was no time. Then the inconsiderate nurse expected me to move myself from the bed to the delivery table. Was she nuts? If I couldn't write, how could I move my overblown body from one horizontal position to another? Somehow, the impossible got accomplished.

Soon, a healthy, but small, baby girl slid out and was retrieved by the nurse, who did nurse things to her. The doctor said something about expecting a much larger baby since I had gained so much weight. Then he continued his tasks by palpitating my abdomen with what felt like boxing gloves. "Please stop. That hurts," I pleaded.

"Just hold on a bit. You know the placenta has to come out, or it will cause an infection," the doctor said. He focused again on the task at hand, and then he said, "Oh, my God! Here comes another one!"

Yes! Small, but healthy, Baby Girl B arrived just four minutes after Baby Girl A, and both within two hours of my first contraction. She was also retrieved by the nurse who did more nurse things. Then the overly cheerful (for that time of the morning) nurse laid a wrapped baby on each of my arms and asked me if I was happy to have twins. I just lay there looking from one baby to the other. Comprehension was not quite there.

My mother related that the doctor approached her in the waiting room with shaky fingers trying to light a cigarette. "It's twin girls," he told her. Then Mom tried to light her own cigarette with shaking fingers.

That is when the fun really started. While I was serenely sitting in the hospital feeding Baby Girl A or Baby Girl B, I have no idea which, Mom was busy trying to scrounge additional baby equipment and clothes from friends and relatives willing to share.

My job was to find a name for Baby Girl B, because Daddy and I had chosen only one girl's name and one boy's name. That task took three days, and I was proud to have selected a beautiful name. The registration nurse asked, "That is an old-fashioned name. Is she named in honor of a family member?"

I replied, "No, this is just a name I like." Guess who came to visit us that evening? Daddy's Aunt (Baby B's first name) who reminded me that her younger sister's middle name was Baby B's middle name. She was so honored that I agreed this was an intentional choice, not a coincidence.

Mom's other job was notifying Daddy of the births. She visited the American Red Cross office which sent a telegram to his military unit. The next day, they called Mom to tell her that Daddy could not be found and was thought to be missing in action. To be sure, they sent a second message by another route. This telegram was confirmed, and Mom could once again breathe easily. There was no way that she was going to tell me that he was missing in action.

Three days later, I received a letter from Daddy. Panic was evident in his pen strokes. "Do we have two babies or four?" He had received both telegrams.

Going-home-day had its own excitement. An aunt was holding one daughter while my mother held the other. Big brother, having been told that he had two baby sisters, burst through the front door and ran to see the babies. He stopped at the first baby and said, "Hi, Sissy," then turned to the other and again said, "Hi, Sissy."

As if on cue, first one baby girl cried, followed by the other just seconds later. Big Brother looked from one to the other, said, "Uh-oh!" and ran to his room. A new toddler-sized football eased his fears somewhat, but he never recovered from the shock. It affected the relationship with his sisters the rest of his life.

When my dad asked who was holding which baby, Aunt replied, "This one, because she's holding that one."

Oh, the other mom in the labor room? She was giving birth to her eighth baby! I took comfort that I only had three children.

As for the twin girls, now they look after me as well as their children and grandchildren.

And me? This great-grandma has many play dates with each of the five little boys, who are the lights of my life.

The Ruse

"Sandy, will you come over tomorrow and help me weed the garden? With all this rain we've been having, the weeds are bigger than the flowers."

"Sure, it will give us a chance to talk without the guys around. Actually, I appreciate the invitation. I'll be here alone. Jim and his brother Randy are going to look at cars. Our old car is beginning to need repairs, and Jim wants me to have transportation he can trust. What time should I be there?"

"How about noon? We can have a light lunch then work. The shade is on that side of the house in the afternoon, so it will be more comfortable to work then."

"Sounds good," Sandy said, just before hanging up the telephone.

Noon – next day: Sandy arrives at her sister's house in jeans and boots, work gloves stuffed in her back pocket and a sagging straw hat perched on her head.

"Come in. Did Jim and Randy go look at cars like they planned?"

"Yes. They left about an hour ago, shortly before I did. They said they were going to check out the new models as well as some nearly-new used ones."

"I hope they choose something you like. Before we go inside, let's walk around back to see the project."

As they approached the back yard, Sandy said, "I think I smell hamburgers."

"You do. That's what we're having for lunch."

"SURPRISE!!" came from behind trees and shrubs as Jim, Randy and the women's cousins jumped out to hug Sandy. It was the moment she noticed a table piled with brightly wrapped gifts.

"What's this? My birthday is next week."

"We know, but it wouldn't be a surprise if we did this on your birthday!"

Reflections

My Greatest Honor of Military Life
A tale of family service and sacrifice

For as long as I can remember, the military has been a part of my life, sometimes actively, and often in the background. That awareness and the pride I feel have always been present, and I know it will continue to affect my outlook on life. What follows are a few of the major events of my military life that have impacted my thought processes and decision making.

***

Born in February 1946, I am one of the original baby-boomers. While our fathers and mothers who served in World War II seldom talked about those days, everyone could see the pride in the way they stood a little taller with glistening eyes as they saluted the flag during Memorial Day programs.

On the rare occasions when they would talk about the war, they told funny things that had happened or a thoroughly sanitized version of other events. A constant presence in our home was Dad's trunk. It was seldom opened, but I knew it contained memorabilia from Dad's time in The War and I was to stay out of it.

One "dark and stormy night," his unit took refuge in an abandoned German mansion which had been well stocked with expensive liquor, cigars and devalued Deutsch Marks. For a few hours, they enjoyed a taste of luxury in the midst of violence and misery as they enjoyed the high-quality cognac and lit those cigars with 1,000 DM bills!

An unbreakable rule in our house was that we did not watch any television shows or movies about war. Dad never went hunting after the war. Mom would often comment, "Dad had a nightmare again last night." Even when he was suffering with dementia, the nursing home aides would report, "Mr. Dillon had a bad dream last night."

My left leg did not develop during my infancy. Mom said it would be still while I moved my other three limbs strongly in my crib. Upon reaching the crawling stage, I would maneuver my left leg on top of my right and go wherever I wanted to go in a 'three-legged' crawl.

When I reached the age that I should have been walking, my parents took me to the doctor who told them to start saving for a wheelchair, because I would never walk and soon would be too heavy to carry. Dad declared, "The hell she won't!"

He picked me up and stormed out of the office. He began massaging and moving my leg for long periods each day. Mom said that my little legs would turn red and I would cry in pain. She begged Dad to stop hurting me, to which he would reply, "Do you want her to walk?" Of course, she did. Six months later I walked into the doctor's office.

Only within the last year have I realized that Dad was doing the same physical therapy on me that had been done to him when he was recuperating in an English hospital after being shot in the hip. He carried that shrapnel the rest of his life. Sitting for long periods was painful to him.

Along those lines, he told us how toilet paper had saved his life. A common practice was to carry a packet of toilet paper in that small space above the helmets' webbing. He had obtained an extra packet, so his helmet was packed with toilet paper, raising it a tiny bit higher than normal. Within a few hours a shot blasted the top of his helmet, leaving him stunned, but intact, thanks to the toilet paper.

***

During my senior year in high school, I worked in a small department store after school and on Saturdays. In the early '60s, stores were still closed on Sundays in Ohio. One afternoon, a tall young man came into the store and asked for help purchasing a Christmas gift for his sister with whom he was staying. I showed him several items. He made his choice and left. During our brief conversation, I learned that he was on leave from the Army to visit his family.

Each day he would come into the store and visit me and the other clerks until he got the evil-eye from the owner. After a few days, he invited me to a movie, and I accepted. Later I learned that two of my coworkers followed us to the theater to keep an eye on us. When they saw that he didn't do anything inappropriate, they accepted us as a short-term couple. As Christmas neared, he travelled by bus to visit the rest of his family in West Virginia. He returned a few days later - too soon, I thought. We had a few more dates, and soon it was time for him to return to his post. He mentioned marriage a few times, but I thought I had made it clear that was not an option.

When school resumed after the holiday, a classmate congratulated me on my engagement. Stunned, I asked what he was talking about. He responded that Orville was saying all over town that he was going to marry me. I wrote to him and told him that I didn't appreciate his telling our business around town, and, more importantly, marriage was out of the question because I was going to college.

As the months passed and I realized that college was not going to be a financial reality, I agreed to marry Orville. In January 1965, he returned from Germany. We had a tiny wedding and made a quick trip to West Virginia so that I could meet his family. They welcomed me without reservations.

A few days later, we loaded my rickety car and began our trip across country to Fort Sill, Oklahoma. We made it as far as Missouri when a semi-truck hit the car and demolished it. I had minor cuts and bruises. Orville was uninjured. We salvaged our personal belongings from the car and rode a Greyhound bus the rest of the way. We rented a tiny duplex in Lawton and settled into married life. A coworker gave him a ride to work every day. I was responsible for laundering his fatigues and polishing his boots. I loved exploring Lawton, the fort and surrounding area, and I even enjoyed camping without a tent. Soon we purchased a cheap, used blue Plymouth, and Orville learned to drive.

I learned how to shop in the commissary and exchange and that no matter where I was, when I heard "Taps", I must stop the car until the last note finished. Those on active duty would hop out of their cars and stand facing in the direction of the main flag pole and salute sharply.

Wanting to do more than sit in our two-room duplex, I began asking about volunteer options. I had been a Brownie and, through high school, a Girl Scout, so that was my first preference. Soon a major's wife knocked on my door and offered me an opportunity to work with a troop. I was excited and eager to work with her. As our conversation progressed, I complained mildly about not being able to afford better housing. She looked me squarely in the eye and said, "If the Army wanted your husband to have a wife, they would have issued him one." That seemed cold and hurtful, yet as the years passed, I realized that she had a valid point. Military life is heart-

and-soul rewarding, but it is also mentally and physically demanding for the active-duty soldiers and their families.

As the months passed, we were hearing more and more about Vietnam and knew that soon Orville would be going. That hastened our decision to start a family. We both wanted a child just in case.

In the first week of August, we packed our well-used car and drove to Fort Carson, Colorado, where a battalion was forming for Vietnam. The commander had strongly recommended that families not accompany the soldier because the length of their relocation was uncertain. Yet Orville wanted me there as long as possible. We found an apartment and lived there only two weeks when the commander ordered that all families must be gone and the soldiers back on duty within two more weeks.

We headed east, encountering more adventures along the way. Our rickety blue Plymouth died along the road. Mom and Dad wired us $500. We bought a blue Ford and resumed our trip. Soon we were back at my parent's home, then made a fast trip to West Virginia to see Orville's family and then returned to Ohio so that Orville could fly back to Colorado Springs. Fortunately, my cousin was a ticket agent for United Airlines and made the flight arrangements.

Shortly thereafter, the new battalion Orville was in boarded a troop train to Fort Ord, California, where they would begin their journey by sea to Vietnam. As they neared their destination, the train was halted because protestors were sitting on the tracks. The train sat there more than a day until the tracks were cleared. Finally, after all paperwork had been processed and inoculations received, the soldiers boarded a ship for one of the last ocean voyages going to the war zone. Within several months, all troops were travelling to and from Vietnam by air.

Fortunately, Orville was not assigned to a combat unit, but to Cam Ranh Bay, a huge beach area. He described it as "the world's largest sandbox." They built an air field and a base while supporting combat troops. Because of his crazy work hours, Orville seldom got to the mess hall at meal times, so he requested bi-monthly care packages.

The following March, our son, Dan, was born and brought big changes to our lives, as all babies do. In August, Orville returned from Vietnam. All too soon he left for his new assignment in Karlsruhe, Germany. Quarters were not yet available, meaning that the Army wouldn't pay for my and Dan's transportation. I agreed to stay behind until quarters would become available, but Orville insisted that we go as soon as possible, even though we would have to pay for the flight. He found an apartment "on the economy," meaning in a German community, and sent for us.

My first ever flight was from Columbus, Ohio, to New York and then to Frankfurt with an infant in arms. By the time we arrived, I was feeling a bit under the weather, so a young soldier carried Dan off the plane and into the airport. This was my first experience of the Army taking care of its own.

Our apartment was unusual to me, but it was normal for Germany. We took warm baths thanks to a hot water heater that burned very expensive charcoal briquettes in the bottom. I had to heat water on the stove to wash dishes and calculate Fahrenheit degrees to Centigrade whenever I wanted to use the oven.

About a month later, quarters became available. Had we waited that short time, the Army would have paid for our transportation. Orville had to go to 'the field' for training, while I moved our meager belongings to fourth floor quarters by taxi. Not yet being familiar with Deutsch Marks nor the German language, this was an experience to remember. As I struggled up to the fourth floor, carrying Dan and as much of our belongings as I could, a neighbor noticed and volunteered to watch Dan while I continued carrying our few possessions up to our quarters.

Just about that time, French President DeGaulle ordered NATO out of his country. That meant that thousands of families were moved from their quarters to unassigned housing in Germany. We offered our second bedroom to a father, mother and infant. The mother spoke only French and didn't like the food I prepared, but we managed until they found a place to live. Not long after that, a family with two small children moved in with us. Since the mother spoke English, we got along well until they found housing. Soon we purchased our first new car, a blue VW Beetle, our first car with front seat belts, and we began to explore the area as much as we could on the number of gas coupons that we were allowed.

Before long, Dan began showing signs of digestive distress. When it didn't cease, I took him to the doctor, who told me that "something in the water" was affecting babies. It was obvious that Dan would begin failing rapidly if he continued to consume the local water. Orville refused to send us back to the States for the next two years. He applied for reassignment, which would only be approved if he volunteered to return to Vietnam. He did. By this time, I was pregnant again. Preparing for the trip, I went to the exchange and purchased square disposable diapers while Orville arranged to have our car shipped. We flew back to the U.S. and travelled from Fort Dix, New Jersey, to West Virginia by bus. When we arrived at his mother's home, Orville's sister offered to watch Dan while I unpacked. Soon she was back demanding, "Haven't you heard of Pampers?" (No, I had not. They had not made it to our exchange yet.) She explained what Pampers were, and I insisted Orville find a way to get me into town so I could buy some. What a difference!

After visits with both families and finding an apartment in Ohio for Dan and me, my cousin once again came to our rescue and made flight arrangements for Orville for transport to Fort Lewis, Washington. A few months later, our identical twin daughters were born. That story is told in "Twins, Oh No!", in this book. Taking care of newborn twins and an 18-month-old, hyperactive toddler was an adventure!

Orville was assigned to the Mobile Riverine Force, meaning that he lived on a LST (landing ship tank) that cruised up and down the Mekong River. These provide ammunition and other supplies to the swift boats that would tie up along-side. He also mentioned retrieving bodies, both U.S. and Viet Cong, out of the river. On one occasion his ship was shelled, but I didn't know this until he returned home and showed the film he had made of the damaged ship.

He reported that soon after arriving aboard ship, he moved his blanket and a few belongings to the ammunition hold. Returning to his bunk each night was not worth the effort, because the swift boats tied-up for resupply any time of day or night. He could serve them faster by being there when they arrived. Again, I sent care packages every two weeks.

During this tour, events kept everyone nervous. In February 1968, the Tet Offensive by the North Vietnamese was decimating both the South Vietnamese military and ours. No mail was delivered in either direction for more than two weeks. In April that year, Dr. Martin Luther King was assassinated, and then in June, Senator Robert Kennedy was killed. Both deaths sparked riots that damaged many cities. My personal fear was that the world was coming to an end.

Orville returned on the day of my grandfather's birthday party. The local news article the next day was more about Orville's return than Grandpa. That seemed odd to me, yet I was pleased that he was honored. Once again, Orville received orders to Germany. He called his senator and explained the water quality issue in Germany and that we now had three small children who could suffer the intestinal distress that made Dan so ill. The senator agreed to investigate the situation. He soon informed us that we would be going to Fort Hood, Texas.

Orville went there first and decided not to live in quarters. He purchased a house in neighboring Copperas Cove. This move was quite the adventure. We still had the blue VW Beetle with no air conditioning that we had purchased in Germany. That August when we began the trip, I filled every nook and cranny and a car-top luggage rack with cribs and other equipment needed to care for three small children until our meager household goods would arrive by van. Luckily, the children were small, so I was also able to fill the space below their feet in the back seats. I drove while my mother kept a close watch on the children. The girls were in what passed for baby seats back then, and Dan sat between them. Each time their little faces began to turn red from heat, Mom alerted me. I pulled to a stop as soon as I could. We took them out of the car and walked around until they cooled enough for us to resume our trip.

Upon crossing into Texarkana, we stopped for gas. Mom and I looked around and began laughing. Across the street was a farm stand featuring a large table full of watermelons. The sign above read, "*Cucumbers.*" When we finally stopped laughing, we agreed that, indeed, "Everything is bigger in Texas." Later that day we arrived at my aunt's home in Buffalo, TX. She asked to change one of the babies. She smoothed the Pamper out flat and asked for pins! I laid that one aside to wipe up future spills and demonstrated how Pampers worked. She was as impressed as I had been the first time I saw one.

Living in Copperas Cove was almost like living in quarters. Everyone on our block and many in the town were military. Children were everywhere. The best part was that there were enough teens to find a babysitter on the rare occasion we treated ourselves to a movie date. One memorable experience is recounted in the story, "A Halloween to Remember," in this book. With three pre-school-aged children, I became well acquainted with the post medical facilities as well as the commissary and exchange.

One rainy day, some neighbor boys were playing in our house. They tied Dan from shoulders to feet with a jump rope and carried him to the kitchen to show me their handiwork. They stood him up. He crashed to the floor and let out a blood curdling scream. I picked him up and untied him. Holding him on my lap, I asked, "Dan, can you stop crying for just a moment so that I can see what hurts." He stopped, and blood began pouring from his chin. One of the boys ran home and returned with his sister who agreed to watch the girls so that I could take Dan to the ER at the Ft. Hood hospital. Dan had still not shed another tear.

The medical assistant said, "Dan, I need to give you a shot so that we can fix your chin. It will sting a little, but if you don't cry, I'll give you a sucker." Dan replied, "Give me a sucker, and I won't cry." The assistant gave him a sucker, and Dan didn't cry. When he finished, the medic stood there amazed and gave Dan a second sucker. I wonder if the medic is still telling this story, too? Looking back, I can see that this was an indication of the Marine he'd grow to be.

One sunny morning, I happened to look out my front window and noticed an Army sedan parked in front of a neighbor's house. I needed no explanation. Her husband had been killed in Vietnam. While I felt grief for her, I also felt relief that the car wasn't in front of my house.

We had lived there three years exploring the area and enjoying the warm winters when once again Orville received orders for Germany. Since the girls were now three years old and Dan almost five, we checked with the post pediatrician who said that their bodies were developed enough to avoid the problems Dan had experienced as an infant. During this pre-move leave, Orville made an agreement with my dad to sell our Volkswagen. It was the same blue as his Buick. When people in town would ask about it, my dad would say, "Our Buick had a baby."

The next question was how to control three small children in multiple airports. We bought walking harnesses and persuaded the girls that they were horses and needed to pull me wherever I wanted to go. We lectured Dan about not running off until we were hoarse and his ears were tired of hearing us call after him. When we approached the airport's military loading area, we had to pass through a security scanner. The guard told me to go through first, then the children, one at a time.

Finally, it was Orville's turn to walk through. BEEP! Take off your jacket, perhaps the brass buttons are setting it off. BEEP! Take off your belt. BEEP! Take off your shoes and shirt. BEEP! The officer in charge was called. In the meantime, the people in line behind us were getting restless, and I was embarrassed to be the cause of this delay. The officer told Orville to step through again. BEEP!

He laughed and said, "You're a farm boy, aren't you?"
"Yes."
"Walk through again taking baby steps."

He did. No beep. As he was redressing and the other people were rushing through the scanner, the officer explained that Orville's long steps caused his fly to gap open and the brass zipper set off the scanner. He then instructed the operator to lower the scanner's sensitivity a couple notches.

That trip went well, and, to our astonishment, first-floor quarters were ready for us. This began an amazing three years of exploring and making new friends. One low cost way to entertain the children on beautiful summer Sundays was to drive to a nearby, bombed-out castle that had overgrown with grass. The grounds were kept mowed for people to picnic, hike and climb. We drove the kids to the site and let them run as long as they stayed in sight. After they ran off their pent-up energy, we had snacks and returned home.

Then came the event that impacted the entire world. Orville and I had treated ourselves to a rare evening of bingo at the NCO club. Just as we finished supper and the games were beginning, an announcement came over the loudspeaker, "Everyone assigned to - - Battalion report for duty immediately." This was not unusual because units frequently held impromptu alerts to test readiness. A minute or so later we heard, "Everyone in - - Battalion report for duty." By this time everyone else in the room was getting antsy, but staying in their seats. Then we heard, "All active duty report to your units, and all dependents return to your homes. This is an USAREUR wide alert."

On the drive home, we tuned our car radio to AFN, Armed Forces Network, and heard that terrorists had killed several Israeli athletes during the 1972 Munich Olympics. That event led to several days of restricted travel and everyone being glued to AFTV, our single English-language television station. After a few weeks, life returned to almost normal. For the next year or so, we dependent adults would be shopping or at a social event and hear an announcement, "Report to school to pick up your children. There has been a bomb threat."

My parents visited us for several days. Mom was shocked the day we went to the exchange. We ran into a friend who bubbled excitedly, "We just got the news. We can stay here two more years." Mom just couldn't imagine anyone being excited about living in a foreign country for five years. She thought vacations were nice, but not living there.

During their stay, we decided to drive up to Nürnberg to visit the Kristkindl Markt, the Christ Child Market, an outdoor Christmas shopping extravaganza. The fastest route was to travel cross-country for several miles, then catch the Autobahn. As we drove on a curvy, narrow country road, we began climbing a hill with a church at the top. My dad began looking around, then exclaimed. "I marched up that field in 1944!" He offered no more explanation.

In the evening we arrived in Nürnberg and checked into a hotel. That late in the evening, only one restaurant was still open, a lovely Chinese restaurant. The menus arrived written in Chinese and German. Fortunately, the head waiter and I both spoke limited German. I managed to order chicken and rice for everyone, except my son who was a bit car sick. The waiter said he would take care of him. Soon Dan was enjoying a delicious bowl of noodle soup that soothed his distress. I remembered that incident several years later when I worked in downtown Chicago around the corner from a Chinese fast food restaurant. Whenever I felt queasy, I went there and was cured with a bowl of noodle soup.

The next day we ventured out to the Kristkindl Markt but didn't stay long. The temperature had dropped over night and we weren't dressed for it. All seven of us piled back into our blue VW Super Beetle and headed home.

Is it any wonder that the next day I had to take my mother to a German doctor for severe neck pain? For some reason, the infirmary declined to see her and said that we should take her to a German doctor. That turned out to be a fortunate incident. The doctor and his nurse both spoke excellent English. After a brief examination, he prescribed her a bottle of liniment that eased the pain almost immediately. She took that bottle back home with her and used it sparingly until it was gone. She tried to buy another bottle, but none of the pain specialists she visited knew what was in the "magic elixir," They recommended this liniment and that, but none worked as well.

Soon our three-year tour was up, and we were reassigned to Fort Lewis, Washington just south of Tacoma. Orville and I were excited to see a part of the U.S. that we hadn't seen before. Excitedly, we broke the news to the children who were then in first and second grades. They listened to the news, thought a moment and asked, "Are there castles in the United States?"

"No."

"Then, we aren't going." We tried to encourage them by reminding them that they would get to see their grandparents and have new adventures.

"No castles. We're not going."

After several minutes of attempting persuasion, the situation dawned on me. "There are forts there, just like in the cowboy movies you watch."

Their ears perked up, and their determined posture relaxed a bit.

"What if we stop at the first one we see?" I asked.

"Can we explore it?"

"Yes."

"Then we'll go."

That settled, we began the process of clearing quarters, making travel arrangements and notifying the folks at home that we'd be dropping in for a visit. Orville sold our blue Super Beetle to a newly arriving soldier.

***

This trip was easier. Orville remembered to take baby steps going through the scanner, and the children were old enough to entertain themselves. We visited as many relatives and friends as we could fit into our short time. Needing a new car for the trip to Fort Lewis, we discussed what kind of car to buy. My only criteria were that it must be large enough for the children to be comfortable and any color but blue. Dad and Orville headed out for a day of car shopping, returning late afternoon with a blue VW Dasher. After expressing dismay about the color, I relaxed and learned to love that car.

The usual leave events occurred, visiting relatives and friends in both Ohio and West Virginia until time to begin our cross-country trip. On the third day, we arrived at Fort Kearney, Nebraska, and kept our promise to let the kids explore the first fort we found. That day was cold, damp and windy. The interpreter, shivering in her shawl (and long johns, I'm sure) gave us, her only visitors, the grand tour while the children ran across the parade grounds, in and out of buildings and up to the ramparts. When they slowed down a little, we graciously thanked our hostess and proceeded to the car.

By the end of the next day, we were ensconced in the Fort Lewis Lodge while our quarters were prepared. We were there a couple of weeks. Once in school, Dan joined Cub Scouts and the girls attended Brownie meetings. I served on the Cub Scout troop planning committee and did a short stint as a Brownie Day Camp leader.

Fort Lewis and the surrounding area were breath-taking. Every place we lived had been beautiful, but here I could step outside my house each morning and determine what the weather would be. If I could see the top of Mount Ranier, the weather would be great. If not, we'd have rain.

We were there a little more than a year when Orville received orders for Guam. By then our marriage had fallen apart. It had been disintegrating for several years, but now it was past the stage of repair. Husband transferred to Guam, and the children and I moved back to Ohio, not my first choice, but seemingly the best option. He got the blue Dasher. I got the used, blue Dodge station-wagon. Once our divorce was granted, I had to surrender my ID card, but the children retained theirs. That enabled them to visit military doctors and shop on base. That privilege was a life saver for a single mom with three children and a low-paying job.

We spent a year there. The teachers weren't quite sure how to handle children who had attended military-operated schools in Germany and Washington. However, being typical military children, the teachers did not need to worry. The kids settled in without problems.

The next year they started school year in Johnson Creek, Wisconsin, a village of about 1,000 people. I had met John, an active-duty, career-Army man who was teaching at a nearby military academy. Within days, I had a job at a factory that manufactured milking inflations. I didn't care for the job but had fun explaining it to non-farming people. On the other hand, my farmer uncles were pleased that I was now in their line of work. Within a few months, I took a job working for the state of Wisconsin. I worked in several different jobs in five different cities over the next twenty-five years. It wasn't long before our blue station wagon died of old age. I replaced it with a tan VW van and have never owned another blue car since.

By the time the children were in sixth and seventh grade, I moved us into a three-bedroom apartment in Watertown, eight miles to the north of where we had lived. Of course, this meant changing schools again. The only problem was that the school didn't want to accept their international immunization records, because they were different than what that school district required. We had a couple contentious telephone conversations, especially after the school system representative suggested that I have the children re-immunized. At that point, I said that international supersedes local, and if she didn't accept their records, I would go to the school superintendent. Once that issue was resolved, we settled into a new work/school routine.

A few years later, John retired and accepted a job teaching ROTC in Gary, Indiana. I transferred to the Wisconsin Tourist Information office in the Chicago Loop. We lived in Whiting, Indiana. Since the kids were in 9th and 10th grade, I promised them that I wouldn't change jobs until they graduated high school. The kids had never complained, but they were pleased to know they would not be changing schools again.

The day we went to register, we ran into the basketball coach, who took one look at them (Dan was 6'2" and the girls were 5'10") and pleaded, "Will you be on my basketball teams, please, please?" They declined but chose to run cross-country for him. We explored that area by driving to fun runs frequently so they could keep in shape for cross-country. If the kids weren't running cross-country, I often travelled with John's rifle team to out-of-town meets where they always came home with blue ribbons. The kids and I cheered his drill team as they competed and won major awards.

We liked the people in that area, but we couldn't seem to adjust to the odors emanating from the oil refineries and the facility that processed corn. In the meantime, I commuted to downtown Chicago by train, bus or van pool as the options became available. This meant long work days of ten hours or more.

***

In the blink of an eye, Dan had reached his junior year and was being courted not only by colleges but also the military. He chose the Marines (See the story, "He's a Marine now, Mom," in this book). He went to pre-boot-camp training events nearly every Saturday where he learned skills that would be tested in boot camp. He would leave for that a few days after graduation.

During his senior year, Dan was an after-the-fact witness to a murder. He saw the killer walking past our house. He was carrying a gun and wearing blood-spattered clothes. Dan told the police what he had seen and was told to be available when the case when to trial.

Months passed. Graduation arrived. My parents travelled from Ohio for the big event. Dan went to a friend's party and came home with his head shaved. That friend and Dan had been through pre-boot camp together and would be leaving the same day for Camp Pendleton, California. They and their friends had been drinking and decided it would be a good idea to get the haircut out of the way before they left. My reaction was not so good. While I accepted that he would be going, I wasn't ready to see the evidence. The next few days flew past and soon Dan was gone.

We wrote often. He wrote less often. The first few times Linda and Sarah drew happy faces on the back of their envelopes. Soon Dan wrote, "No more happy faces or anything but my address and your return address. Anything else earns me punishment." During a forced march, Dan collapsed from heat exhaustion and was sent to the hospital. The Marines recommended immediate discharge. Dan must have been at his persuasive best, because they allowed him to stay.

While in training for his job as a computer programmer/analyst, the murder trial became scheduled. The court contacted his unit and arranged a 24-hour leave. He flew from San Diego to Chicago. The next morning, I drove him to court. He testified. We had lunch and returned to the airport.

Dan was sent to Camp Smith on the island of Oahu, Hawaii, after completing several training sessions at Camp Pendleton and Quantico, VA. His room overlooked the Battleship Arizona. He was there during Operation Desert Storm and experienced an unusual situation. He worked in a six-person shop, and five were sent to the war zone. Dan had to maintain the shop by himself during the day. At the same time, Marines transporting from the U.S. to Iraq received further training at Camp Smith. During the eight-plus weeks of the war, Dan was acting Sergeant-of-the-Guard protecting those transition troops. He lived on coffee, chocolate and cigarettes, and, at most, he got an hour or two sleep each night and just occasional meals in the dining hall.

On a lighter note, Dan related the story of the time that he was called into the commander's office and told that he would be escorting the commander's daughter to the Marine Ball. He said that he enjoyed the evening but added, "The hard part was showing her a good time, but not too good a time."

Several years later, Dan left the Marines and came to live near J.R. and I just outside Madison, WI. He met Linda B., one of my dear friends, and they became a couple. He graduated from Madison Area Technical College and began working as a programmer-analyst. This was the same work he did in the Marines but with entirely different equipment and programs, thus necessitating the additional schooling. After working in Madison a few years, he accepted a job in Virginia, Minnesota, up in iron country, not far from the boundary waters. In July 2011, I flew to Wisconsin and met up with Linda B. We drove to Dan's mobile home and spent a few days there. He took us the see the local sites and to enjoy the magnificent North Woods.

That November, Dan drove down to West Virginia to visit his father and family. He shot and butchered his first deer while there. Then he drove to Williamsburg, Virginia, to spend time with those of us living here. After several days, he drove back to West Virginia and then returned to Minnesota. A week later he had a fatal heart attack.

My daughter Sarah and I drove to Wisconsin, connected with Linda B. and continued on to Minnesota. His employer welcomed us, gave us Dan's keys and arranged for us to stay at a company-owned condo at a local ski resort. The next day, we drove to Dan's house and began the job of sorting his belongings. Since Sarah's Army job was in personnel, she was assigned to go through his military papers and decide what needed to be kept. I took his bedroom and office. Linda B. handled the rest of the house. Over the next several days, we laughed and cried together as we sorted, chose a few items to keep, took his clothes to Goodwill and disposed of items we deemed to be trash or recyclable. Fortunately, the owner of Dan's mobile home was an on-line auctioneer. He sold everything that remained and sent me a check. Sharing this experience helped us work through our grief.

I was privileged to receive Dan's flag. It sits on top of my bookcase next to my father's flag.

***

Meanwhile, Linda and Sarah were being courted by the Army. Again, graduation came all too soon, but, luckily, they didn't come home with bald heads. They attended pre-basic training camp, too, but had fewer, less intense sessions.

Preparing for basic training had been simpler for Dan. He had been permitted to take only a tooth brush and tooth paste to boot camp. The Army recruiter gave me a list of personal items that the girls were required to take, including a travel bag, white cotton underwear and toiletry items. That meant multiple shopping trips. Upon reaching their basic training sites, the girls had to put their belongings in storage and were given military issue underwear as well as their uniforms.

Another big issue was their hair. They had grown it down to their waists. A woman friend, who had retired from the Army, strongly recommended that they get it cut short because they wouldn't have time to fuss with it in basic training. Hoping to give them time to acclimate to the new style, I made an appointment at a local beauty shop. They fussed and fumed the whole way there, but they sat stoically in their chairs while internally seething as their beautiful hair was cut into above-the-collar styles. I tried to make it an event by taking before, during and after photos. There are no smiles in those pictures. As soon as basic training was over, they grew their hair long again.

The girls left on separate days. Sarah went to Fort Jackson, SC, for basic training and to Fort Benjamin Harrison, Indiana for training as a personnel specialist. John and I travelled by bus from Indiana to South Carolina to see her graduate from basic training, but we were only able to spend a few minutes with her in the hustle and bustle of the ceremony. Since Fort Harrison was only about three hours from where I lived, I was able to visit Sarah from time to time. She even had a couple weekends off to spend with me.

Linda went to Fort Dix, New Jersey, for basic. I rode Amtrak to see her graduate. She had 24-hours leave before departing for Fort Sam Houston, Texas, to be trained as a food inspector. We toured Philadelphia's historic area and spent the night in a motel near the fort. All too soon I drove her back to Fort Dix and watched her board a bus that would take her to the airport.

***

After training, Sarah reported to Worms and Linda to Bremerhaven, Germany. They were able to visit each other a few times. Soon Linda married Robert, and, months later, I travelled to Bremerhaven to witness granddaughter Jennifer's birth.

I did a little touring and shopping in Bremerhaven. I was interested to note that the locals could not understand the German that I had learned in Baumholder, which was in the portion of the country that had shifted back and forth between Germany and France over the centuries. Their pronunciation was softer with very slight French inflections. So, I adapted and spoke only English while there.

***

A year or so later, Sarah married Jay. He had been transferred to Fort Huachuca, Arizona. She flew there from Germany and they got married in Las Vegas. She returned to Worms and was soon reassigned to Fort Huachuca. They were there during Operation Desert Storm. Sarah cut orders for her cousin to go to Iraq. I was privileged to spend several days with Sarah and Jay and to visit a portion of the country that was new to me. I even visited my cousin who lived near Phoenix.

The best part of these two trips was getting acquainted with my sons-in-law. I could say volumes about them, but I will limit my comment to, "My daughters made good choices."

From Fort Huachuca, Sarah and Jay were next assigned to Augsburg, Germany, where Sarah chose to leave the Army. Jay stayed in until he retired at Fort Stewart, Georgia. They then moved to his hometown of Hampton, Virginia.

***

After Bremerhaven, Linda and Robert moved to Fort Stewart, Georgia, where my grandson, David, was born. In the meantime, I had moved back to Wisconsin. John and I had decided to part. I could not be present at David's birth because I was attending Alverno College in Milwaukee, and David was born mid-semester. Fortunately, Robert's mother was able to be there for his sacred moment. Shortly thereafter, wanting to spend more time with her children, Linda left the Army. Subsequently, Linda and Robert were assigned to Fort Gordon, Georgia; The Presidio, California; Fort Lewis, Washington; Heidelberg, Germany; and Landstuhl, Germany, from where Robert retired. They were there during Operation Desert Storm. Robert was a surgical assistant, helping the wounded who had been evacuated there for surgery before returning to the States.

I had the privilege to visit Linda and the children twice at Fort Lewis. I remembered many locations there and showed them where we used to live. I even introduced them to a Tacoma park where we used to picnic. The park had an antique carousel. Some of the horses had been built by President Eisenhower before he attended West Point.

The first trip was a graduation gift from my new husband, J.R. The second time was after Robert received orders to go to Heidelberg. My mom had never met her great-grandchildren and didn't want to wait another three or more years, so we planned a trip. She drove from Ohio to my house near Madison. We travelled together to Fort Lewis, a three-day journey. Observing new territory (Minnesota, North Dakota, Montana, Idaho and the rest of Washington) was a treat for us.

Seeing everyone again was a joy. Neither of us had yet met Robert. He was "in the field" again, as he was during my first visit. Robert called to say hello. He asked me, "Why do you always visit when I'm gone?" I responded, "Why do you always leave when I plan a trip?" We laughed, acknowledging those things happen when you are a military family. Our trip was over much too soon, and we headed back across the northern plains to Wisconsin, where J.R. had a hot meal waiting for us. Mom stayed a couple more days to rest, and then she drove back to Ohio.

***

Sometime after Sarah and Jay moved to Hampton, J.R. and I flew down to visit them. They showed us all the sights and included a Chesapeake Bay sunset cruise. I so much enjoyed seeing them. Not long after that visit, J.R. and I went our separate ways.

A couple years later, Linda and family planned a vacation to visit Sarah and Jay. Mom and I immediately scheduled flights that would get us there at the same time. At the last minute, we persuaded Dan to join us. What a time we had! Nine of us were packed into Sarah and Jay's small house during the day. Linda and family spent their nights at the Fort Eustis Inn. During our visit, Linda mentioned that Robert was thinking about retiring from the Army. She said that Robert wanted to live near his family in Florida, but she had spent all those years separated from her identical twin and expected to live near her in retirement. Hearing that, I said I would retire to the Virginia area too. Mom said that she would consider it.

***

In 2000, Robert retired, and the family moved from Landstuhl to Williamsburg, where he had been hired as a surgical assistant. Early in 2001, I retired from the State of Wisconsin. In April, I drove to Ohio, picked up my mom, and we drove down to Williamsburg to look for housing. I found a small apartment and moved in early June. Dan drove the rental truck with my belongings. Everyone joined the work team to get me moved in. With all those experienced movers, we finished the job in about an hour. The next day, Sarah and I drove Dan to the Norfolk Airport. He was flying to Africa to meet some friends on a spiritual journey. Ten days later he was back with photos and tales to tell.

Even though I haven't had a military ID card since 1976, I still feel connected to the military through my daughters and sons-in-law. I miss the atmosphere and friendship. Many military people retire to this area in Virginia, which is full of military bases. Using those facilities allows them to live a little nicer life than they would be able to afford in a strictly civilian area. The retirees can also continue to enjoy the military camaraderie. By living here, I can enjoy it second-hand through their stories.

My greatest compliment came when I worked for Aeronautics at the Wisconsin Department of Transportation. My supervisor, a retired USAF pilot, introduced me to one of our military liaisons as an Army veteran. Shocked, I said, "I'm not a veteran. I was just a wife." He replied, "You are a veteran, and so is my wife and every other military wife. You had to pick up the slack, deal with emergencies and care for our children while we were gone, not knowing if or when we might return. You had to comply with rules for military spouses. You are a veteran." The liaison said, "Yes, you are."

    I accepted the designation humbly and with great honor.

He's a Marine, Mom. Be Cool.

The following article written by the author originally appeared in the August 24, 1984 issue of the Chicago Tribune.

Last year when I signed the delayed entry papers, I felt very proud that my son knew what he wanted for the future. I was so glad he had a positive patriotic goal; very relieved that he chose the Marine Corps computer program rather than combat arms training; and disappointed that college was not his first choice.

But a year is a long time and high school graduation so far away. He was, after all, still my child even though he had very adult ideas.

The year passed with many of the usual teen-parent quarrels. But we all found ourselves making concessions to the future marine. For example, on a family trip with only one extra seat in the car, his sisters deferred to their brother because it would be the last time he would participate in this particular activity. Extra money for the prom. OK.

When we asked him why he didn't choose the Army like his father, who retired as a first sergeant, he replied, "Because I don't want anything easy." We didn't feel he was putting down his father but proud that he was seeking the difficult challenge.

On one level, he was being allowed to develop his independence faster than I'd hoped so he would be able to cope without the family. But on an emotional level, we all tried to draw closer because we knew our time was limited. I found myself frequently telling anecdotes about the early years of this soon-to-be man.

As the months narrowed to weeks, I found myself contemplating whether I had taught him the skills he needed as an adult. Did I give him the right outlook on life? Was he prepared to make moral judgments? Would he be assertive enough? Would he be too aggressive? Could he handle the super discipline of boot camp?

Why didn't I spend more personal time with this precious son? Those 18 years God gave me to impart knowledge to this boy were all too short. A year ago, his future seemed so far away. There was plenty of time to teach and love. I also felt closer to my mother, because I knew her parting was harder. She had only one child.

I found myself telling others, "I'm too young to have a son in the Marines," or, "No I'll have to change my own light bulbs." I had to make a joke of it for myself as well as for others. No one wants to hear a mother fret about her firstborn leaving home.

All too soon graduation came, and what gift is appropriate or someone who is leaving home and can take nothing but a toothbrush? Days were spent searching for an appropriate gift for a traveling man to be used after boot camp.

What do you give a person to be used three months hence? We couldn't bear to have the traditional part. So, it was just us and the grandparents. Besides, he would be attending many other parties that week.

Only a few days left, and he calls for a ride. "Sure, son, I'll be there in a few minutes." A couple months ago he would have been advised to take the bus. I'm not a taxi service. But with three days to go, he can ask, because I secretly hope he wants to be with me as much as I want to be with him. And why did he have to get that haircut now? Couldn't he wait until he had to get it cut? Aloud, I tease him about his ears sticking out.

The big day comes, and he throws a peck on my cheek as he runs out the door. Is that all? But I wanted a bear hug like he gave me on Mother's Day. "Don't forget, Mom, he's a marine now; he has to be cool before his friends," explains my daughter.

Two days ago, the MARS operator relayed the message that he had arrived safely and reported his address. Did it take me a full minute to find a tablet and pen to get a letter started? I find myself stopping to look at his photo on the wall. It is no longer just a feature of the décor but a bond between mother and son. And though I say how nice it is to have a smaller grocery bill, when will I be able to look at his empty place at the dinner table without a sigh?

In three months my son will be home—a Marine standing tall in his new uniform. How proud I'll be that "me and gunny taught him everything he knows." Will these three months go by as quickly as the past year? When will be the next time I'll see him after that? Will the Marine Corps send him to a hot spot on the globe?

On arising, my prayer is no longer, "Give me strength to do what needs done today," but "Lord, take care of my son."

Daughters Tackle the Army

A year after their brother joined the Marines, my identical twin daughters left home to join the Army. I didn't write an essay about their departure, and this disappointed them. When they asked why, I told them the truth: The stories would have been almost identical except for writing daughters instead of son and Army instead of Marines. Now I can look back and write what I was unable to say back then.

I was so proud of my girls choosing the Army both to serve and to learn a usable skill. Yet I worried about them differently than I had my son. I knew they could surmount whatever challenges they faced in basic training, but as girls they were much more vulnerable in so many ways than their older brother was. Because they chose different job specialties, one a food inspector, the other personnel manager, they went to basic and advanced training at different locations. These two girls, who had functioned almost as one entity for 17 years, were now forced to be individuals relying on themselves.

All I could do was trust God that they would be safe. As far as I know, they were, but I also know they still hide unpleasant facts from me. Whatever they faced, they became strong women. As they matured, both married career Army men. Both men were good choices. One daughter gave me a granddaughter and grandson. In turn they have given me five great-grandsons so far. The other daughter has become a close friend and support for her stepsons and their families.

These women have been my cheerleaders and caretakers, and they provide me strength, motivation and wisdom. They encouraged me when I went to college, they supported me when I faced life-changing decisions and they cheered me during down times. They monitor my health and support me when my spirit is low. Best of all, I feel that they do it out of love rather than duty. Sometimes I think that is more than I deserve. Even so, I am very proud of them and brag about them every chance I get. Most of that bragging is vocal, but it's long past time to put those words in writing.

So, I'm taking this opportunity to say, "Linda and Sarah, I am so proud of you. You've become strong women who exemplify all that is honorable and compassionate. You are role models for younger women – and for me. I trust your words and actions and probably rely on you more than I should. Thank you for gracing my life."

Thirteen Days in the Twilight Zone

Recently, I packed my car, drove to Norge (a village outside Williamsburg, Va.) and picked up my granddaughter, Jenn. We were heading to West Virginia for a family reunion. We planned to be gone three days: two days to travel and one for the reunion. Jenn's two sons rode with her parents who are my daughter and son-in-law, Linda and Robert. Lunches were packed, and music was set to play automatically while we drove. Both cars used the same computer-mapping service so that we could easily find each other if we became separated.

The trip went well for the first few hours. Jenn and I chatted about this and that: books, movies and the boys, while old-lady music played in the background. Soon we were on U.S. 33 crossing into West Virginia. The road was very curvy but in good shape. Some portions were two-lane, others were four-lane. Because the route changed rapidly from curvy to straight, the speed limit varied from 15 to 60 mph within minutes, even though it sometimes felt like seconds. Fortunately, both Jenn and I had taken Dramamine to deal with the dis-orienting mountain curves before starting the trip.

By mid-afternoon we reached Buckhannon, a small city which is home to West Virginia Wesleyan College. The city is old, but new stores such as Wal-Mart are moving into the area. We checked into the local Microtel and then followed Linda and Robert and the boys across town to catch State Route 20, a curvy two-lane road that winds through some villages and rural areas. After several miles, we reached Alton Road, a county road paved in the last five years or so. Here we faced two-way traffic that appeared to be one and half lanes wide (in my flat-land eyes). We eased ourselves up the mountain at a pace just fast enough to keep the engine from stalling. As we encountered experienced drivers coming downhill, we held our breaths, even whispering an occasional "Our Father" before we exhaled.

Suddenly, a truck loomed over us as we entered a curve. I pulled to the right and slipped off the road's edge. Coming back onto the pavement, I heard the thump-thump-thump sound that could only mean one thing. I eased back onto the gravel shoulder and set the emergency brake when I stopped. Seeing the right front tire detached from the rim, I knew that I was not going any farther.

Knowing that Linda, Robert and the boys had been just a short distance ahead of us and that they were on the alert, Jenn and I tried to think hopeful thoughts as we stood by the disabled car. Soon, indeed, they were back to assess our situation. Robert left and took Jenn and the boys to our relatives' farm while Linda attempted to remove the damaged tire. She didn't succeed because the gravel berm was not firm enough to support the jack. Besides, it was narrow, and I feared that one of us might inadvertently fall down the steep incline of the mountain. So, I drove the car back onto the pavement enough that the jack could be successfully implemented. Once the wheel was elevated, we could see that the front rim was sheared in half. It took a while, but we managed to remove it and install the "donut" tire. The corresponding back tire appeared to be fine, so we began the last leg of our journey, another couple of miles up Alton Road.

The dreaded sound returned: thump-thump-thump. I pulled to the edge again. This time, a quick glance revealed that the back tire was shredded and that the rim was dented. Once again, Robert and Linda returned to the crisis scene. Since cars come equipped with only one "donut", Linda drove the car a few yards onto a pull-off for the mail truck. This additional delay brought relatives who looked over the situation, pondered the options and offered advice. The consensus was that it was now 5 p.m. on Saturday and that repair shops would be closed. The best option was to let the car sit until Monday morning. So, we headed up the road to the family farm. There we had a delicious supper and nice visit with our closest relatives. These included my former husband (who was my daughters' father), his wife, their children, an aunt and his son's-in-law father).

With the help of the West Virginia gang, we all made it back to the hotel for the night and back up the mountain the next morning in time for the reunion at what appeared to be a nearly-deserted-country-church property with picnic tables and swings. The day started with an abbreviated worship service followed by prizes for the youngest, oldest, most newly married, etc. Everyone was in a good mood, laughing as they asked, "Who are you?" and "Do you remember?" We then headed to the pavilion where mounds of food welcomed us. We ate and visited under tall shade trees while the children played. I am thrilled that even though I'm no longer legally a part of that family, I'm welcomed as a family member.

After the reunion, we returned to the farm. Other relatives joined us, and we enjoyed a huge picnic on the deck. Soon, it was time to caravan back to Buckhannon and the hotel.

Early the next morning, I called AAA for towing. They said that they'd be there in a few hours. I checked out of the hotel. Since I had to wait for towing and repair, the relatives took me, Jenn and the boys back up the mountain, while Linda and Robert drove around town trying to find a garage to replace the rims and tires and get us on our way. The relatives told us not to trust Jenkins Ford in Buckhannon, but I didn't know if AAA would pay for a tow to Clarksburg, the next closest option which was another hour away. I do have long-distance towing, but right then I wasn't thinking clearly. So Jenkins Ford it was.

Jenkins had neither the tires nor the rims to fit my car: a 2012 Ford Focus, a nice generic car. The parts manager said that he'd order the parts that day. The next day was July 4th, so the parts would be shipped on the 5th and arrive on the 6th, and then I'd be on my way. My insurance company offered a rental car, so I could come home, but the family consensus was that, rather than make two long trips, I should stay put for those three days. A three-day vacation sounded good, so I agreed. Robert, Linda, Jenn and the boys headed back to Williamsburg. Because we were so far from Buckhannon, I could not send or receive cell phone calls, but I could text. I sent my supervisor a text to alert him that I'd be gone for longer than I planned. Being the kind person that he is, he wished me luck for a fast and safe return.

The small farm house had an extra bedroom that was up an extremely steep staircase. No one wanted me to fall during the night, especially me, so we agreed that I would sleep in the mobile home next door. The daughter, son-in-law and their two daughters lived there. I was willing to sleep on their comfortable recliner settee. After all, I frequently fall asleep in my own recliner. There was only one problem – access to the bathroom was through their bedroom.

That meant that any night-time trips I required involved putting on shoes, walking across the deck and walkway into the house to use that bathroom and then returning to the trailer. I didn't mind, but 71-year-old bladders don't have an early warning system.

Otherwise, the time was spent amiably. We all got to know one another better, becoming friends and sharing memories and hopes for the future. I already knew they were nice people, but I didn't expect them to be as welcoming and caring as they were. They fed me well and made sure that I was comfortable. They gave me a tour of the farm's many acres of woods and crops, and we made trips to Buckhannon and Clarksburg (me with Dramamine's help) just to break up the routine. I met a hydroponic gardener and learned how that process works. I had fun playing with the children. Now, I'm looking forward to our next visit – as soon as I can figure out how to get up a mountain with my car intact. Even better, maybe they'll drive to level ground where I live.

Thinking I'd be driving home on the 6th or 7th at the latest, I decided to plan my return trip. I did not want to travel US 33. It was much too curvy for my comfort. I chose to drive home via the interstate system. That is a little longer but much easier to drive. I knew I-64 would take me from Charleston to Williamsburg. I just needed to know how to get from Buckhannon to Charleston.

I asked for and received a paper highway map. Everyone declared, "Don't mess with that. Use your phone."

I responded, "I prefer the old-fashioned method."

As I unfolded the map, my former husband began punching buttons on his phone. I studied the map and noted my routes and where to make changes and then returned the map to the person who gave it to me.

Ex-husband said, "Here's your route. Do you want to make notes?"

"Don't need to. I'm already done. See my notes?"

"How did you do that so fast?"

"I used to do this for a living."

However, on July 6th the car saga extended. I called Jenkins Ford and was told that only the tires and one rim had arrived. The other rim would arrive in another day or so. We all took deep breaths to remain calm and accept the situation. But on the 8th, no rim; on the 10th, no rim; and on the 12th, no rim. I asked to speak to the parts manager. I telegraphed my frustration clearly, explaining my situation. He apologized but said there was nothing that he could do about the delay in receiving the rim. I replied that I would call the Ford corporate office to express my distress. He chuckled and responded that I could do that if I wished.

I did wish and called the Ford corporate office, leaving a message that summed my situation and noted the parts manager's dismissive attitude, including the fact that I had missed six days of work, was imposing on my relatives, that my employer was getting upset and that I had run out of prescription medications days earlier.

Early on the 13th, I called again and was told that, hopefully, the rim would arrive that day. I was so frustrated that I decided to return home - car or no car. I tried to reserve a rental car in Buckhannon. No car was available. I then called Clarksburg. They would have a car ready for me at 11 a.m. I reserved it. The daughter and son-in-law drove me to Clarksburg. The trip to Clarksburg included an emergency stop because I had forgotten to take a Dramamine tablet. When I got to the car rental agency, no car was available. After reminding them that I had reserved a car for 11:00 and that meant one should have been available, they said that one would be available at 2:30 p.m. that afternoon.

We piled back in the van to return to the farm. On the way, I remembered that I had left my house keys on my car key ring, so we stopped at Jenkins Ford in Buckhannon to obtain the house keys. I told the clerk that my car was there and I needed my house keys. She said, "That car?" and pointed into the repair bay. I replied, "Yes." She said that the repairs were just then finishing!

With a sigh of relief, I paid my deductible and a fee to keep the rim that had been sheared in half. Soon, we were transferring my luggage from the van to my car, and by 1:30 p.m. I was on my way home, finally.

Did my call to the Ford corporate office help? I don't know, but I like to think it did.

I drove a short distance on Hwy 20 and turned onto US 33 West. As soon as I made that turn, I could feel the stress leaving my body. I was on my way home!

Before long, I was on I-77 South to Charleston, then on I-64 East to Williamsburg. I arrived home at 9:30 p.m. and sighed with pleasure as I walked into my house. Early the next morning, I drove to my job and was relieved to learn that they had not replaced me.

Because of all the delays and the parts manager's seeming lack of concern at my distress, I decided that I would discuss the situation with my own Ford dealer. I took my car to Williamsburg Ford who reviewed all the repairs and assured me that they were done correctly. To my extreme gratitude, they did not charge me for checking that the repairs had been correctly done. They said they had no idea what could have caused the delay in receiving the rim, but they explained that sometimes aluminum rims shear and that I must have hit something more than the gravel when I drove off the edge of the road. That's very possible. I had been too distressed that first day to notice if there were other debris in the gravel area.

Finally, I'm breathing normally and anticipating my trip to North Carolina next month. However, I plan to do a lot of meditating before I begin driving up the mountain that leads to the retreat center. If I successfully navigate that trip, I may be ready to tackle West Virginia again.

End note: The trip to North Carolina went smoothly except for a 22-mile-stretch with one-lane-directed traffic on I-85 for road repairs. Traffic through those zones at times slowed to 5 mph and, occasionally, even stopped for several minutes.

Believe me when I say, "At the first rest stop after traffic returned to normal, I had to stand in line."

The next big question is, "Will I tackle West Virginia again?"

I think so, but I plan to drive the interstate system!

Meant to Learn

"No part of your experience is wasted. Everything you've experienced so far is part of what you were meant to learn." - *Martha Beck**

The first several times I heard words similar to that quote, I scoffed. There is simply no way that I was meant to experience the terrible and boring parts of my life. I was meant to be beautiful, smart, rich, athletic and other wonderful adjectives.

Let's see what really happened. Freckles were the bane of my existence when I was younger. Now I consider freckles as part of my distinctive appearance, adding a little flair to my pale complexion.

I was a very smart student, but smart is relative. Facts are wonderful to know, and they help us in many ways, but understanding how relationships work is a greater gift.

Like many young women, I learned about relationships through reading novels and observing my parents. My parents obviously loved each other, but their love didn't look like what I read in books. They never had the privilege of expressing their feelings with gifts. Now I realize that Mom expressed it when she cooked a meal that my dad liked rather than what she would have preferred. Dad expressed it when he took Mom for a drive just to get her out of the house for a couple hours.

Mom showed her love by sewing new outfits for me when she could afford the material. I thought I should have clothes from expensive stores. Later, I learned that she looked through magazines to learn what was in style, selected a similar pattern and made a garment with much less expensive fabric.

Both parents expressed their love for me by being very strict. Not having the freedom or the "things" many of my friends had made me jealous. Now I realize that their rules kept me out of trouble. However, these also made me rebel and marry the first man who asked me – just to get away from their rules.

Athletics happened only in my dreams. The stereotypical kid who gets picked last was my reality and well deserved. I now realize that my body was just not designed to be lithe, graceful and quick. I accomplish most things I want to do, but sports is just not one of them. One good thing about this is that I've never had a broken bone.

As an adult, I joined a local softball league. My coach and other team members were patient and kind while assigning me to play right field (of course). After the last game of the season, our coach told me he was proud of my determination despite my several injuries. I thanked him and explained, "My doctor told me to take up this sport for my health." We both enjoyed a good laugh at the irony. He's probably still telling that story to his coaching buddies.

I have to brag about my one success that season. One evening, our team was short of players. With a sigh of resignation, my coach assigned me to third base. Amazingly, I caught the ball and tagged out the opposing runner. The whole team cheered.

The last adjective, rich, is still elusive. I've worked hard and have done well in my jobs, but I haven't accumulated wealth or a contingency fund. On the other hand, money comes when I really need it. For example, an uncle passed and left me enough to pay off college debt. My son transitioned a few years ago. His insurance was enough to make repairs on my house, replace my old car and pay for necessary dental work.

The more important type of wealth has been free-flowing and loaded with intangible benefits. My parents obviously loved me, even though I was an ungrateful child. My two marriages did not work out well, but I learned a lot about how I relate to others and what kind of treatment I deserve. That knowledge serves me well. While my jobs didn't pay well, they were all interesting and taught me much.

My real wealth comes from my family. My son was hard to control and his actions incomprehensible to this girl-child who feared to step out of her parents' rule book. By being a unique individual, my son learned much about life, and he taught me many of his lessons.

My daughters are gifts from heaven. They share their lives with me and allow me to spend holidays and to have "just fun" days with them. Sometimes I get frustrated that they don't share their problems with me. But I realize they are protecting me from stress that is not mine to carry. They go to doctor appointments with me and take notes. Then they check to be sure I'm following the physician's advice.

Additionally, they gave me two wonderful grandchildren who, in turn, have given me five great-grandsons, each one unique. The boys are allowed to spend days with me, one at a time, of course. They keep me young, playing cars, tossing a ball or watching "Captain Underpants." Is there anyone who cannot laugh at that movie?

Love and laughter are the glue that hold life together, make pain bearable and heal all wounds.

*Martha Beck's Daily Inspirations, September 11, 2017, info@marthabeck.com

The Way to Start Changing

"The way to start changing your mind is not to force it or command it, but to watch it."
- *Martha Beck**

This quote immediately swept my mind to January 1. Many of us, woozy from "too much party" the night before, sit at a table, pen and paper in hand, making a list of our New Year Resolutions. We resolve to work out at the gym every day to tone up our sedentary bodies and lose 25 pounds by March 1, to give more to charity, to be kinder to the neighbors and to save money for a new car. We know the list. We also know how soon it will evaporate into the ether. We've been making the same resolutions annually - for how many years? Our determination quickly falls by the wayside with all our other obligations and unexpected events. So why do we go through this process each January? We are trying to force a solution to our perceived shortcomings.

Another example is when the coach tells us to practice an hour a day. Yeah, right. How long does that last? Professional athletes do this because going to practice is in their contract. We also know that they had determination from childhood. So how did they succeed, and we don't? They found something that was so important to them that they wanted to excel, and to be great they had to practice. They noticed that practice made their bodies stronger and their efforts more effective.

However, for the rest of us, most of our decisions to change don't have that much impact on our daily lives. We just want to look good or to be nicer. These are ephemeral goals. A better way to tackle those goals would be to say, whenever we happen to think of it, "I'd like to have a healthy weight for my height." If we try that approach, we'll likely notice that we are saying, "No, thank you," to the cookies by the office coffee pot. Sometime later, we'll realize that we are walking during our lunch period instead of chatting with co-workers. Perhaps, a co-worker or two will join us on our walk. Then we notice that we were having such an interesting conversation that we walked an extra block without realizing it. As a result, we see our waist bands getting looser and our shirts staying tucked. This may even inspire us to try the gym and find a coach.

The same goes for those other "unreachable" goals: charity, kindness and saving money. We say to ourselves, "I'd like to be more generous, kind and frugal." As we think those thoughts about how we'd like to act, we find that it happens:

One day we send a $5 check to the food bank and then maybe $10 to animal rescue. On a cold, rainy morning we pick up the neighbor's newspaper and place it next to their door. Later, they thank us for our kind deed. We find ourselves dropping our change into a jar and watching it grow. After several weeks we take it to the bank to exchange it for dollars. We've just made a good start to on the holiday gift budget. This year, maybe we can pay cash instead of amassing credit card debt.

Once we notice small changes, we can see that we've grown and can feel better about ourselves. Then, instead of worrying about our shortfalls, we will take pleasure in our improvement. That pleasure becomes the incentive to keep taking those actions to become better people day by day.

*Martha Beck's Daily Inspirations, October 2, 2017, info@marthabeck.com

Thoughts on Playing

For the earnest student, taking responsibility means never forgetting to have fun.
Play if you want to be responsible. - *The Universe**

Reading this message felt like a ray of sunshine lighting my being. Like most of us, I often take life too seriously. I fret over bad news, and this affects my enjoyment of the remainder of the day.

Terrible things that we can't prevent happen to people. Our country has recently been hit by three destructive hurricanes, wild fires, floods and murders. We can do nothing to stop these horrendous events. They are part of nature and life and will come whether we want them to or not.

How we react to those events is what is important. If trained, we can do rescue work, restore utilities, offer medical assistance or any of the many other tasks involved in assisting our friends, relatives and neighbors. Others of us can donate goods or money toward the rescue efforts. Still others of us have various limitations that prevent active participation. I'm one of those people. So, I assist by volunteering to work at local blood drives, registering donors and offering them treats when they are finished. Those tasks feel like play because I meet so many wonderful, giving people. Additionally, I'm fortunate to be a universal donor, so I donate on a regular basis.

Of course, those of us with limitations often have the most intense job of all. We are asked to pray for the safety and well-being of everyone involved in the disaster, whether victim or rescuer. Everyone can use the mental, physical and spiritual support that prayer offers. We don't have to spend hours in intense meditation. Each time we have a thought about the event, we can send up a quick, silent request for those involved.

Today's quote reminds us that we must play. Life should not be all serious thoughts and serious work. There are many ways to play: participate in a sport, push a child on a swing, hike in the woods, swim, read, or watch a movie. This list could go on and on. There are as many ways to play as there are people on Earth.

Earlier today, I pulled dead flowers and some weeds from my yard. Yes, that's hard work, but it was a joy to my body and spirit, just to be able to enjoy the fresh air and know that my body is still capable of doing this task; albeit, in short spurts. I can no longer work for hours in the garden, so several brief exertions make the task pleasurable. After using my muscles in an unaccustomed task, I came in the house, enjoyed a cool drink and then relaxed into a short nap, feeling grateful for the fresh air flowing into my house from the mild autumn weather. As I awoke, the sound of hundreds of birds chirping, tweeting and squawking thrilled my soul. I sat silently in my chair enjoying the music for the few minutes it lasted. The migrating fowl must have completed their short rest break and resumed their travel south.

I play at work. I'm fortunate to work at a theme park and two local historic sites. Each day I have the pleasure of meeting visitors from around our country and the world. In a few minutes we learn about each other and become instant friends. Their joy in visiting a new place matches my joy in sharing information and learning something new.

Another way that I work and play is by reading my morning newspaper. I can hear you exclaim, "She still gets her information from a newspaper!" Yes, I do and here is why. A newspaper provides reports from multiple sources, allowing me to read several points of view about a single event or person. After I dutifully read the news, I reach the fun section. You know the one I mean, the comic pages. I luxuriate in giggling at the antics of my favorite cartoon characters, and then I solve the day's puzzles. Some are easy, some require me to think, and still others are beyond my ability. Those last I ignore because working them would not be playing.

Those of you who have read my essays know that my favorite way to play is with my five great-grandsons, who range in age from 1 to 10. Each one has a unique perspective on life and play. A few days ago, the seven-year old was talking about his great-grandfather. He started to say, "Grandpa," but then he quickly changed it to, "You know, your old husband." I laughed so hard that I could barely maintain control of our car. When I caught my breath, I assured him he could refer to that person as "Grandpa."

Returning to the quote, I will just say that play is not just fun. It is also a tension reliever and a way to make new friends. It almost always gives us a new outlook on life and our responsibilities.

TUT – A Note from the Universe, October 5, 2017, theuniverse@tut.com

Energywriter is…

When I see an unusual email or blog name, I wonder about the story behind the name. Some examples in my address list are: bleedgreen, jadespirit, stageit, starscape, feedpanthers and dunpayn. Some are easy to figure out. Others are more difficult, leading me to ask what influenced that particular word-number combination.

In the same vein, several people have asked, "How did you come up with *energywriter*?" Easy, actually. You know that I'm a *writer*, or, at least, I think I am. But *energy*, why?

I have studied and practiced energy healing since 2000. For years before that, I suffered fibromyalgia and those "itis" brothers. You know who I mean – arthritis, bursitis, and tendonitis. Several people suggested that I learn how to do self-Reiki to ease my pain. I said, "I'll check on it," and continued taking pain pills. Of course, nothing changed. I continued to complain and feel helpless.

In 2000, my son took a Reiki course and asked if he could practice on me. As he worked, I felt an energy spiral running from my sacrum to the top of my head. At the same time, I saw a rainbow of colors. When he finished, I said, "Sign me up for the next class." He did, and I was running toward a new way of life that included physical activities which I had had to bypass for several years and new ones such as volksmarches (5 or 10 - kilometer organized walks).

Even though we learned how to treat ourselves in the first level, I yearned for something that could help others also. I continued studying level 2, master practitioner and even master teacher. These classes were not inexpensive, but worth every dollar. I learned how to treat people and pets. Even better, I learned how to treat long distance.

As I travelled this road, I learned about other healing modalities such as body talk, healing touch, cranial-sacral, aroma therapy and many others, all fascinating. I have experimented with Reconnection, Quantum Touch and Transfigura-Regeneration, a Belgian modality.

What does all this have to do with energy? Everything is energy. Even what we perceive as solid is moving energy. If you doubt this, an easy way to learn is by reading Greg Braden's books. He translates into ordinary language complex scientific facts as presented by Albert Einstein, Nicolai Tesla and Max Planck.

How does this work? That's harder to explain. Since all energy comes from Source/Universe/God, it is everywhere and available to everyone. A practitioner asks to be a clear channel for Universal energy to flow through her to the client. The practitioner never asks for a specific outcome. Instead, she intends that the energy will be used for the client's highest good.

Why so many different modalities? Basically, they all work the same through intention and free-flowing Universal energy. The differences are that methodologies used vary according to the individual's client's needs. Each practitioner finds the healing style that suits him or her. Sometimes a client needs to try different modalities before healing takes place.

I know that sounds contrary. If they are all similar, why doesn't one work as well as the next? It is because each person has a different energy vibration and needs to find a healing method that resonates with his or her body and mental/emotional state.

About the Author

Sharon's second book, *Gemstones and Dimes,* is a compendium of several writing genres. She includes humorous stories, fiction and thoughtful, serious essays varying in length from short one-pagers to several pages. Her stories derive from her life experiences and topics that she considers worthy of discussion or may provide a few laughs.

The stories in Sharon's first book, *Echoes of Your Choices*, mark her journey through the turbulence and vicissitudes of ordinary life. Compassion and forgiveness of self and others are themes underlying this journey. She demonstrates that life must be fun as well as serious and spiritual as well as practical. Her lessons view the world and the people who inhabit it through a wide-angle lens.

The author has been a reporter and feature writer for several newspapers and magazines in both Wisconsin and Virginia. Presently living and working in Virginia, Sharon is a member of local and regional writers' groups, a frequent participant in the Erma Bombeck Writers Workshop and a member of the National Society of Newspaper Columnists. She recently received the Rick Baily Humor Award at the annual Chesapeake Bay Writers luncheon and author recognition event in Williamsburg, Virginia.

Her treasures are her family members and friends, especially her daughters, grandchildren and five great-grandsons. "Those boys keep me active and curious. In other words – young," Sharon explains.

You can purchase *Gemstones and Dimes* and *Echoes of Your Choices* through Amazon, Barnes and Noble and other on-line booksellers. If you prefer an autographed copy, you can purchase the book from Sharon by contacting her at energywriter@cox.net.

www.ingramcontent.com/pod-product-compliance
Lightning Source LLC
Chambersburg PA
CBHW060537100426
42743CB00009B/1555